Reflections on the Qur'an
A Ramadan Reader

Reflections on the Qur'an
A Ramadan Reader

Mohamed Hag Magid
Hanaa Unus

Sterling, Virginia, USA

Fourth Edition 2013

ISBN: 144990324X
EAN-13: 9781449903244

Cover photo by Sanaa Unus

Printed in the U.S.A.

This book is dedicated to my teacher's father,
Hag Magid Hag Musa,
whose wisdom and knowledge continue to touch so many.

And to my father, Iqbal Unus,
whose dedication and encouragement made this book possible.

Hanaa Unus

Note about Fourth Edition

This fourth edition of the book includes exercises that follow each surah or group of surahs, besides some editorial changes from previous editions.

Readers are advised to work as many of the exercises as possible with each reading, do so together with their families when possible, and maintain a private journal to record their responses to the exercise questions.

Contents

Preface

This book was inspired by a young man who approached me one Ramadan and said that he loved the recitation of the Qur'an but that he did not understand the meanings of the recitation. This motivated me to make the meaning – and understanding - of what is recited in taraweeh easily accessible to people in the congregation. As a result, we sent by email each day a summary of what was going to be recited that evening. These summaries were well received by readers not only in the local community but also in many parts of the world. I thank that young man and make du'a for him. His remarks will bring benefit not only to those who listen to the Qur'an being recited in Ramadan but also to those who read it on their own.

I am also grateful to the All Dulles Area Muslim Society (ADAMS) community which has established a custom of learning and understanding the Qur'an by studying the tafsir of a few verses in sequence every morning after Salat Al Fajr. Regular attendees at the Fajr sessions have had the opportunity to have studied the tafsir of the entire Qur'an in this manner.

I am grateful to my assistant Hanaa Unus for the long hours and late nights that she has worked to bring this book into existence. I also appreciate the editing assistance of Nasim A. Khawaja. I also thank Dr. Iqbal Unus who suggested the idea of the book itself and helped in compiling and publishing it as an easy reader.

May Allah reward them all.

Mohamed Hag Magid

Introduction

The Qur'an was revealed in the blessed month of Ramadan. Its revelation is honored by this beautiful month. The Qur'an rekindles the hearts of the believers and their desire to heed the words of Allah (swt). In order to maximize the deeper connection that should be built each year with the Qur'an, we should focus and maximize our efforts to study this beautiful book.

Allah says in Surah Al Qamar, verse 17: "And We have indeed made the Qur'an easy to understand and remember: then is there any that will receive admonition?" And in Surah Muhammad, verse 24, Allah asks: "Do they not then earnestly seek to understand the Qur'an, or are their hearts locked up by them?"

The Qur'an, as a book of guidance, comes to answer the ultimate questions: Why are we here? Who brought us to where we are? Where are we going? The subject matter is about each of us as human beings, defining our relationships with Allah Almighty, defining our relationship with one and other, and defining our relationships with the rest of the universe. Failure to reflect on the Qur'an leads to disconnect between the divine revelation and us. Unfortunately, the Qur'an is treated often only as a book of *barakah* for a new home, a marriage, or being recited at the funeral to bring comfort.

But the Qur'an is much more than that. Every verse calls us to action. The Prophet Muhammad (peace be upon him) lived the Qur'an. When his wife, Aisha, was asked about his moral conduct, she replied, "His moral conduct was the Qur'an."

It is the Qur'an that calls us to be the Ummah of witnesses (2:143).[1] Those who read the Qur'an with reflection

---

[1] Thus, have We made of you an Ummah justly balanced, that ye might be witnesses over the nations, and the Messenger a witness over yourselves; and We appointed the Qibla to which thou wast used, only to test those who followed the Messenger from those who would turn

will find in this beautiful book the answer to any question they have. As the Qur'an has a holistic approach to human life, it does not define anything as one-dimensional. For example, when the Qur'an talks about humans, it explains the biographical aspect of the human being as well as the psychological, emotional, and social aspects. Sadly, the Muslim Ummah has created obstacles and barriers between themselves and the Qur'an. Many people think that the Qur'an can only be approached by imams, sheikhs, mullahs, and scholars, forgetting that the Qur'an was revealed for all of mankind. We should remember that the Prophet Muhammad himself was an illiterate orphan. This is why clergy, in the Islamic tradition, do not exist as they do in other religions, where the interpretation of the text can only be given by the elite. The Qur'an speaks to all people of every background and level of knowledge. There are a select number of Qur'anic verses regarding rulings that should not be interpreted by individuals, as they require specific technical skills and knowledge. But these verses are very few. The remainder deals with principles that govern human life and those are for everyone. An example is that of Surah Adh Dhariyat, verse 56, in which Allah (swt) talks about the purpose of creation: "I have only created jinn and men, that they may worship Me." These verses do not require deep interpretation for us to understand the meaning. The concept of worship is clear in this verse and we use such verses as a criterion in fulfilling that role in our lives.

Living in a country where Arabic is not the native language, many amongst us may depend on the translation. We encourage American Muslims to study the language of the Qur'an so they can gain direct access to Allah's words. While we all work on this, we should try to find the most accurate translation to read because, again, the Qur'an is not a book exclusively for any one group of people. It is not a book only for

---

on their heels (from the Faith). Indeed it was (a change) momentous, except to those guided by Allah. And never would Allah Make your faith of no effect. For Allah is to all people Most surely full of kindness, Most Merciful.

the Arabs, so do not put it aside because you do not know the language of the revelation. Benefit from the translation while you study the original language.

This is why we took it upon ourselves to compile these summaries. We hope that these summaries will allow those who attend the Taraweeh prayer to understand the infinite beauty of the words being recited each night. There is nothing that can reveal all the jewels of the Qur'an, but this is an attempt to simplify its meaning and let the light of those jewels shine a little each night.

The splendor of the Qur'an is the collection of all the aspects of life and connecting limited life to the infinite nature of God and His power over all things. Allah shows us these connections throughout His book, so we should make it a habit in our lives to reflect on His magnificent creations in order that we may live harmoniously with the vast universe and all that is in it. As you will see in this book, we try to summarize the major themes of every surah of the Qur'an in order to encourage you to read the lessons of each surah ahead of the imam's recitation.

In conclusion, we would like to share with you what Imam Ghazali considers an important element in helping a person reflect on the book of Allah. Imam Ghazali explains in his book, *Revival of the Islamic Sciences*, the inner dimensions of the recitation of the Qur'an. He made important points to have in mind when approaching the Qur'an:

1. We must understand the significance of the words of the Qur'an as the divine words of Allah, Most High. Therefore, every word, every verse, every surah, is a representation of His infinite wisdom. Imam Ghazali gives the example of the sun, that is raised above us but it is not with us. The distance of the sun from us allows us to benefit from its light and warmth, but if it were with us, we would certainly be overwhelmed. Through His infinite knowledge Allah gives us what fulfills the need of His creation so that we can complete our

purpose, but protects us from those aspects of it that we cannot bear.

2. A person should realize from whom these words are coming. This means that we need to learn about our Lord and understand His greatness as the Creator and Sustainer of the universe. It is Allah that has infinite wisdom, power, and knowledge. Great scholars like Imam Zain Al Abidin from Ahlal Bayt of the Prophet Muhammad (peace be upon him) never used to say, "I heard the Qur'an say..." Rather, he said: "I heard Allah say..." It is important to make the connection between the words we are reading and hearing, and from what source they came.

3. Allah (swt) reminds us in the Qur'an to take this book seriously and to exert effort and strength to comprehend His words. Imam Ghazali calls upon us to contemplate and reflect on these words with an open heart and an open mind.

4. Reflection comes after the presence of the heart, when a person takes a moment to prepare the self to approach the Qur'an with a pure mind and heart. He suggests reading a verse more than once. The Prophet (peace be upon him) used to repeat verses or recite them more than once for the purpose of reflection.

5. Imam Ghazali also talks about the importance of *tadabur* and *tafakhur*. Tadabur is to actively reflect on the words of Allah. Tafakhur is to draw lessons out of the Qur'an. He gives examples throughout the Qur'an, asking if we see His signs—like the changing of night to day, bringing life to the dead earth, and the destruction of entire civilizations that deviated from the truth. Such signs allow us to understand the concepts being presented as well as the truth of the words of Allah.

6. We must take away things that come between individuals and the Qur'an:
   a. A person should try to recite Qur'an correctly. We all make mistakes, and perfect recitation is

something that takes time to master, but we should put forth the effort to come as close as we can to reading the words of Allah correctly.

b. We should try to recite or read Qur'an in an environment that is conducive to deep reflection. This does not mean that, if you have children, you should not read when they are around. You can read and allow them to play around you even if they make some noise. But take 10 extra minutes before they wake up or after they sleep to read a few more verses and reflect quietly on the meanings and lessons of those verses.

c. Avoid committing great sins. This is the case in all aspects of our lives, but sin is an obstacle in the path to understanding the greatness of the Qur'an. Therefore, it is putting the weight of a great sin on our scale as well as setting hurdles in our way to coming closer to Him (swt). We should seek forgiveness before approaching the book of Allah.

d. Read a summary or a translation in your primary language so that you can understand the context. Some people have difficulty with Qur'anic vocabulary. Acceptance is good, but understanding what you are reading is needed in order to truly accept.

7. Personalize the Qur'an by believing that every word is personally for you. Although it may talk about other people through stories and lessons, Allah has intended His words for all of us, as He (swt) says in the verse 44, Surah An Nahl(16).[2]

8. *Ta-athur* is the impact of the Qur'an on a person's life. We need to think about what transformation has

---

[2](We sent them) with Clear Signs and Scriptures; and We have sent down unto thee (also) the Message; that thou mayest explain clearly to men what is sent for them, and that they may give thought.

resulted from our interaction and reflection with the Qur'an. In the verse 29 of Surah An Najm, Allah (swt) says: "Therefore, shun those who turn away from Our Message and desire nothing but the life of this world." Allah (swt) is emphasizing the great importance in making changes after reading His words. In Surah Al Anfal, verse 2, He says: "For Believers are those who, when Allah is mentioned, feel a tremor in their hearts, and when they hear His signs rehearsed, find their faith strengthened, and put (all) their trust in their Lord." These are the people who have internalized the signs of Allah and take them to heart. When we hear the commands of Allah and we hear reference to His signs, these should bring a complete conversion of our mind, body, heart and senses to those things pleasing to Him (swt). Our goals, and our actions that may get us there, should all be aligned with what He has decreed as permissible. Our goals should never involve us in compromising what He (swt) has forbidden us from doing.

9. *Taraqi* is the elevation of a person moving from different stages in recitation. The lowest level is when the servant recites the words of the Qur'an back to Allah (swt). This makes a person humble and in the state of *khushu'*. The middle level is when a reader feels that Allah (swt) is addressing him or her. Finally, the highest level is when the reader sees Allah (swt) as the speaker of these blessed words and heeds them as a result of that.

10. *Tabari* is the last level of interacting with the Qur'an. Imam Ghazali meant that when a person comes to understand and know the Qur'an, they are endowed with an illumination of power and knowledge by submitting completely to the divine.

"Say: If the ocean were ink (wherewith to write out) the words of my Lord, sooner would the ocean be exhausted then

6

would the words of my Lord, even if we added another ocean like it for its aid," (18:109). The Qur'an is like the ocean. It holds knowledge beyond what the eye can see, encompasses more than what the mind can comprehend, yet the power of each wave can be felt deep within the heart. We invite you to look at this beautiful ocean of the Qur'an, to immerse yourself in it and—though we will never be able to reach its limits—for all the efforts we put forth we will find its pearls enriching our lives beyond anything of this world.

NOTES

(It may help to make notes and jot down reminders about what you want to pay special attention to before you start reading the chapters that follow.)

1

Reflections on Ramadan

"O you who believe, fasting has been prescribed for you as it was prescribed for those before you in order that you may attain God-consciousness." (2:183)

The month of Ramadan has been honored by the revelation of the Holy Qur'an. The Qur'an was sent down from the highest heaven to the lowest heaven in the blessed night of Laylat-ul Qadr, Night of Decree. Muslims honor this month through fasting. "The month of Ramadan is the month in which the Qur'an was revealed as guidance to mankind and a clear evidence for life," (2:184). Fasting serves as an instrument for gaining nearness to Allah Almighty, and achieving purification of the heart and mind. Muslims look forward to the coming of Ramadan with great longing for the spiritual, physical, and emotional benefits this special season brings.

Ramadan is a month of heightened devotion. In addition to the five daily prayers, we gather nightly for extra prayers. During the last 10 nights of Ramadan, some individuals and even whole families seclude themselves in the mosque for *itikaf*: nights spent performing extra prayers and reading the Qur'an. It is a spiritually intense period of reflection and devotion, whose purpose is to seek guidance and ask for forgiveness, quietly focusing on getting closer to Allah and strengthening the bonds of brotherhood.

Muslims believe the Qur'an holds the cure for ailments of the soul. Intensifying the relationship with the Qur'an renews the spirit to counter what may have seeped through the barriers and entered the heart.

Ramadan is an opportune time to cultivate compassion for others, particularly for the poor. We are urged to be more generous during Ramadan, giving our time, giving our wealth, and giving ourselves. Muslims believe that in Ramadan, the majority of the *shayateen*—jinns who encourage acts of evil— are chained down and prevented from influencing people. As such, Ramadan becomes a time of personal evaluation. Each person knows their deeds and sins; a sin committed in Ramadan cannot be blamed only on the whispers of Satan; rather, it can be attributed to whims and desires that have not been constrained. Therefore, the person must strive to overcome the penetration that Satan has made into the soul of that individual.

A person is not left to his or her own devices to do this. The Qur'an is the medicine for any spiritual ailment of the believer. The Qur'an was revealed as a guide for us in situations of difficulty and in situations of ease. Each person is in a unique state, different from any person around him or her. Yet the Qur'an speaks to each person at his or her own level and encourages growth through practical steps, bringing them closer to Allah Almighty. The Qur'an is also a source of healing for the illnesses of the heart—illnesses such as jealousy, hatred, anger, and envy. Any one of these has the potential to destroy more than just the individual.

Allah reminds us, "Verily, in the remembrance of Allah do hearts find comfort," (13:28). The Qur'an is a source for healing sadness and a reminder that, through kindness and dignity, true happiness can be found in the Life to come.

2

Reflections on Taraweeh

What is Salatul Taraweeh?

"Taraweeh" is the plural of "Tarweeha," which means "to bring comfort to one's self." It is called Taraweeh because the Companions of the Prophet used to pray a long prayer and would then sit between the two rakat to rest ("Tarweeha" is taken from the root word "raha," or "to rest"). Unlike Tahajjud—prayer done during the night after having slept—this Qiyam is made prior to a person lying down to sleep.

The Prophet (peace and blessings be upon him) explained that Allah made it obligatory for Muslims to fast and made it sunnah to pray Qiyam in Ramadan. In another Hadith narrated by Abu Huraira, the Prophet (peace be upon him) used to encourage the Muslims to do Qiyam in Ramadan without ordering them to do so. Whoever prays Qiyam in Ramadan with sincerity and devotion, Allah forgives their previous sins. It is also reported that the Prophet (peace be upon him) prayed in the nights of Ramadan alone in his Masjid. Others came and joined him in his prayers, but he did not initiate the gathering. He did this on two separate days; on the third day he did not come to the Masjid. He later explained to the companions that he did not come out because he was worried that they would make it obligatory on themselves.

The tradition of praying Taraweeh as a group started during the time of Omar (may Allah be pleased with him). He went to the Masjid one evening and found people praying in different groups or alone. So he gathered them and had them pray behind Ubay ibn Ka'b. His decision was based on witnessing people praying behind the Prophet (peace be upon him). Omar was happy with the outcome but also explained that, in the eyes of Allah, Tahajjud still holds preference over the Taraweeh prayer.

What do the four scholars say about Taraweeh?

Imam Malik says that Taraweeh is *nawaful mu'akida* (an optional action that is well established). Imam Shafi explains that a voluntary prayer done in congregation holds greater reward than the voluntary prayer done alone, but also indicates that sunnah after salah takes priority over Taraweeh. Hanbali describes Taraweeh as a preferred Tatawwa' (voluntary) prayer because it is prayed in congregation. It is encouraged that people pray in congregation, but if they are not able to do so, and need to pray at home, the manner of salah is the same.

In regards to the number of rakat to be prayed, Hanbali, Shafi' and some Maliki say Taraweeh is 20 rakat. Imam Shafi indicates that people of Madinah at times prayed up to 36 rakat. Imam Kathani says 20 rakat is considered the consensus (not including the Witr prayer). Due to the length, if a person finds difficulty in standing, it is permissible to sit down in the prayer.

Where can one find the most reward from Taraweeh prayer?

The Maliki *madhab* indicates that it is preferable to pray Taraweeh at home as long as a person does not abandon the Masjid. If you pray at home, encourage everyone in the home to join you if they are able. Hanbali, Shafi and Hanafi prefer Taraweeh to be in Jama'a, or congregation. For those with small children, greater reward may be found in praying at home, if the child is uneasy or distressed at the time of Taraweeh and there is no option for childcare. The reward is no less than what was intended.

While Maliki and Shafi' say that it is preferable for the Imam to complete the whole Qur'an, another opinion of Imam

Malik is that you do not have to complete the Qur'an. The Khatmul Qur'an (completion of the Qur'an) can be done in reading by oneself, and does not have to be done in prayer only. Therefore, if you miss a portion at the Masjid in Jama'a, you can complete it through reading or praying at home.

Maximizing the Benefit of Taraweeh at the Masjid

1. For those not fluent in Arabic, read the English translation of the sections that the Imam will be reciting that evening. This will help you focus on what is being recited and will enhance your prayer.

2. Come to the prayer with the spirit of love and respect for one another by being courteous and considerate of others.

3. Parents should help their youth to be involved in the prayer itself and be part of the Taraweeh experience. If the recitation is too long, pray eight rakat and then return home (especially on school nights).

4. Parents of children: Salatul Taraweeh is not an obligation. If the small child is uneasy during the prayer, we recommend that you pray at home.

5. If you are arriving late for Taraweeh prayers and the Imam has already completed Salatul Isha, you should not pray in a separate group while the Imam is praying. It causes extra noise that leads to confusion. You may pray in another room or you may join the Taraweeh congregation with the intention for Isha. Please remember to stand and complete your additional two rakat of Isha when the Imam completes the two rakat of Taraweeh.

6. Sunnah are not obligatory acts, but Fajr is *Fard*, or

strictly required. If your Taraweeh is preventing you from waking up for Fajr, then let go of Taraweeh and make sure to get up to pray Fajr.

3

Surah Al Fatiha to Surah Al Anfal

Surah Al Fatiha (1)

Surah Al Fatiha is the opening surah of the Qur'an. The title literally means, "The Opener." Some scholars believe that this surah was revealed twice, once in Makkah, for the purpose of Muslims establishing prayer and then revealed a second time when the Qiblah was changed from Aqsa in Jerusalem to the Ka'bah in Makkah. Being one of the surahs of the Qur'an to have been revealed twice, we see the emphasis on its importance.

Surah Al Fatiha serves as an introduction to the Qur'an, covering all the major themes presented in the many surahs that follow it. It is a short surahand the entire remainder of the Qur'an is said to be an explanation of its seven verses. As a result, Surah Al Fatiha is also referred to by the title of Umm al-Kitab (the Mother of the Book).Surah Al Fatiha has many other names; here are a few: al-Wafiyya (the sufficient), al-Kanz (the treasure), and as-Shifaa (the healer). The Prophet Muhammad (peace be upon him) said that the Qur'an is a healer for every disease with the exception of death. This is not to say that we should not seek consultation from professionals such as physicians and psychologists, but this begs the question: why—when we face diseases of the body, mind or heart—do we seek cures in ways that He has deemed unlawful for us?

Unfortunately we see people trying to resolve their feelings through oppression, alcohol, and the harming of life, be it others' or their own. We see people engaging in these actions because such actions either make them think they are stronger or allow them to lose their senses temporarily and avoid feeling pain at all. Turning to such actions to resolve their pain rectifies their situation only momentarily and, even then, only in their minds. In reality, all they need to do is to read the words of comfort that He has provided, and they will find comfort in their hearts. In Surah Ar Ra'ad, we are reminded that, "Verily in the remembrance of Allah do hearts find rest."

Other names attributed with Surah Al Fatiha are Mathani and As-Salah, because of its place in prayer. Mathani means "dual," and there is no prayer (salah) in which it is not recited at least two times. The name 'Surah As-Salah' is due to the fact that there is no correct prayer without the recitation of these glorious seven verses. Surah al-Hamd (Surah of Praise) and Surah Ath-thabit (foundational surah) are other common names for Umm al-Qur'an.

There is no surah whose uniqueness—in terms of its wording and the weight of what it contains—is comparable to that of Al Fatiha, be it in the Torah, the Injil, or in the Qur'an.

Surah Al Fatiha begins with the Basmalah, but there are differing views as to whether the Basmalah is an actual verse of the surah or not. Imam al-Shafi says that it is, while all other scholars say that it is not a verse and, as such, the Basmalah is recited in a silent voice in prayer.

Surah Al Fatiha is a prayer and in it we ask for guidance from Allah (swt). In the immediately following surah, Al Baqarah, Allah tells us, "This is the Book; In it is guidance sure, without doubt, to those who fear Allah," an immediate response to the very prayer made in Surah Al Fatiha.

In a Hadith Abu Huraira reported hearing the Prophet of Allah (peace be upon him) explaining that Allah Almighty said, "I divided the prayers (Surah Al Fatiha) between Me and My servant. When My servant says, "All praise is due to God, Lord of the Universe," I say "My servant has praised Me." And if My servant says, "The Source of Mercy, The Most Merciful," I say, "My servant has acknowledged My attributes and has praised Me." And if My servant says, "Owner of the Day of Judgment," I say, "My servant has glorified Me." And if My servant says, "You alone do we worship and from You alone do we seek assistance," I say, "This is between Me and My servant and I grant My servant what he asks." And if My servant says, "Guide us on the straight path, the path of those who have earned your pleasure and not of those who have earned your anger and your wrath," I say, "This is between Me and My servant and My servant shall have what he has asked for." – Sahih Muslim

From this Hadith, we learn that Surah Fatiha is a direct dialogue between Allah Most High and His servant. This connection was very important in the daily routine of the Prophet (peace be upon him) and should be the same way in our own lives. Prayer is not the only time to recite Fatiha, but it is a designated time to have this dialogue with Allah (swt). If we know Fatiha to be a dialogue and Allah has instructed us to recite it in prayer, how can one refuse the opportunity to converse with our Lord? How can we prefer to finish watching a football game or to chat on the phone unnecessarily when He is saying He is available for us to speak to Him so that He may respond? How can we sleep through Fajr or delay prayers until the last minute? Is there someone more important with whom we are speaking? Is there something He has not provided us that prevents us from speaking to Him? We must look at the reason why we are not more mindful of our prayers and reflect on whether it is really a justifiable reason to miss a dialogue with our Creator and Provider.

Al Fatiha begins with the beautiful Basmalah. In this, as well as in the third verse of Al Fatiha, we reflect on two oft-repeated attributes of Allah (swt). As we hear these two names, the Source of Mercy and the Most Merciful, we should try to understand what He has so mercifully given us and we should try to reflect this attribute in dealing with others. Muslims should strive to spread mercy and kindness toward all life, as Allah has told us that mercy manifests itself in His words. Allah tells us in the Qur'an that He has sent His Prophet (peace be upon him) as a mercy to mankind. Then what is it that causes us to exert mercy and kindness on those outside of our homes, and come home and release all our tensions and anger on our families and those closest to us? Why do we expect mercy from our children but not share mercy with them, or expect kindness from our spouses when we do not act kindly toward them?

Allah commands us to be merciful to one another. As we ask for Allah's Mercy and embrace His Kindness, we need to check our relationships with our spouses, children, and fellow human beings. Allah's Mercy encompasses all that is in His universe and we are nothing more than *His* creation. Therefore, His Mercy is granted to us, and we should be instruments for spreading it to others. Part of Allah's Mercy is that His door of repentance is never closed. As we celebrate this beautiful month of Ramadan, we must make an extra effort to seek Allah's forgiveness. He has invited His servant to walk toward the door of forgiveness with the promise that at any time before death, regardless of our mistakes and shortcomings, this door is always open.

The first verse of Surah Fatiha reminds us that all praise should be directed: to Allah alone. This is the comprehensive *hamd* that includes *shukur*, gratitude. This is to praise Allah and be grateful to Him (swt) in times of prosperity and happiness, and in times of trial and difficulty. This means that we glorify Him for His infinite attributes regardless of our situation at any particular moment. Hamd is to praise Allah for who He is.

When we think about "al alameen," the universe, we have to think about it in terms of all the worlds within the universe that we know and then in terms of the worlds that only Allah knows—the worlds we, with all of our scientific knowledge and tools, may never know. Consider only the world you are aware of and try to locate yourself amongst all of His creations.

At any moment, Allah Almighty can cause any number of these beings, or any one of us, to cease existing. If we reflect on the smallness of ourselves in the vast universe, we feel His greatness when we recite, and we feel the sense that *all* praise truly belongs solely to Allah.

The third verse establishes Allah (swt)'s ownership over the Day of Judgment. It will be a day when we will all stand before him for accountability for the deeds we harvested in this life. The concept of us standing before Allah Almighty is overwhelming and comforting at the same time. It is overwhelming to think about our shortcomings and errors but comforting to know that all the hardship and injustices are brought forth on scales and made evident for how we lived our lives.

After acknowledging the power of Allah in the universe, we must act upon our affirmation that He is the Ruler of the universe and it is before Him that we will stand for judgment. The fourth verse of Surah Fatiha emphasizes in its grammar that the worship being done is for Allah alone and absolutely no one except Him, and that the help being sought is also from Allah alone and no one except Him. Reiterating the sentiments of the previous verses that Allah is the one to whom all praise is due, Verse 4 emphasizes that Allah is the Owner and Sustainer of all the worlds and all that they contain, from whom all mercy is bestowed, and by whom judgment is decreed. Is there any other who would be suitable for us to worship and seek help from other than Him?

We seek Allah's guidance to be on the straight path. The fifth verse uses the word *'ihdina*, meaning not only to guide but to guide and keep us on that way. A straight path is the most direct path from one place to another. Metaphorically, we understand the straight path to be the most direct path to Allah (swt). This is not to say that it is the easiest path. A direct path up a mountain, for example, will be very steep. We know that Shaytan tries to distract us from the straight path by producing opportunities for us in our lives that may seem "easier," like cheating on tests, withholding Zakah when it is due, sleeping through Fajr,etc. He presents these to us as options that are easier for us, but Allah (swt) did not promise a life of ease. Rather, He promises a worldly life of trial, but with that, He pledges that if we stay on the straight path through the trials, the reward of reaching the summit—or Paradise—will more than sufficiently compensate for the struggles faced on the journey.

Exercises for Surah Al Fatiha

1. Learn the dialogue that takes place between you and Allah (swt) when reading this surah. Then recall that dialogue when reciting during prayer. If you internalize that conversation, you will find the concentration in your prayer increased.
2. Reflect on the meaning of Rahma. Then reflect on how you manifest this rahma in your personal life and see what more you can do to exemplify rahma.
3. Use As-Shifa', the Qur'an, when you need healing. Whether the need is physical, spiritual, or emotional, make the words of Allah the first place you turn to for help in times of difficulty or calamity, paying particular attention to the word *Istina*.
4. Reflect on the word Hamd. Do something that helps you put the power of Allah in perspective; spend time looking at the ocean or gazing at the stars. Remember how small you are in Allah's vast universe. Then look at all the blessings He has, by His Mercy, given to you, your parents, spouse, children, home, and everything inside it. Praise Allah for His greatness while expressing gratitude for the blessings for which He has singled you out. That is Hamd.
5. We ask Allah in this surah to keep us on *Sirat Al Mustaqim*. Take 20 minutes at the end of your day to evaluate your actions and behaviors. Evaluate the

benefit in the time you spent with others. Did they lead you towards things that were pleasing or displeasing to Allah? Make corrections accordingly for the next day.

Surah Al Baqarah (2)

Surah Al Baqarah begins with a strong and clear statement that this is the Book in which there is no doubt. Its contents are true and certain. It is the criterion by which to measure ourselves throughout the year, in every action that we take.

Surah Al Baqarah was revealed to the Prophet Muhammad (peace be upon him) shortly after the Muslims' migration to Yathrib, later known as Madinah. The Muslims were building their new community under the guidance of the revelation. While doing this, it became clear that the Muslims would simultaneously have to protect themselves against threats and challenges from those amongst them who showed interest in hindering the establishment of the Muslim community in Madinah. It was during this time of great tension that the lengthiest surah of the Qur'an was revealed—286 verses long. From this surah we understand that Islam encourages tolerance across faiths. Allah will judge us, not on how much we seclude ourselves from the world around us, but on what we do to make it a better world for all those who inhabit it: "Indeed, those who surrender themselves to Allah and do good works shall be rewarded by their Lord; they shall have nothing to fear or to regret," (2:112).

Surah Al Baqarah is unique in the sense that it mentions all five of the principles of Islam: Tawhid, Salah, Zakah, Sawm, and Hajj. Surah Al Baqarah also puts emphasis on fearing Allah, mentioning it over 30 times throughout the surah. He (swt) reminds us to believe in Him and all of His prophets in their role, each as a guide to humanity.

Though Surah Al Baqarah is at the beginning of the

Qur'an as it has been compiled, it is one of the later surahs in revelation. As the belief in one God had been firmly established by the Makkan revelation, these Madinan verses progress toward further providing details of the Islamic law. Surah Al Baqarah covers the details of topics such as covenants, divorce, financial responsibilities, equality, and other matters pertaining to families. However, Allah (swt) brings back the verses regarding His Oneness and reminds mankind that above all, we must remember that Allah (swt) is One alone and no partner should be attributed to Him.

Surah Al Baqarah contains two very unique verses: Ayat al-Kursi, verse 255, and the longest verse in the Holy Qur'an, verse 282. Ayat al-Kursi is the greatest verse of Surah Al Baqarah.[3] It contains a beautiful description of Allah's Greatness and Majesty. Verse 282 is the longest verse in the Qur'an and deals with contracts and guidelines in resolving disputes.[4] The

------

[3]Allah. There is no god but He,-the Living, the Self-subsisting, Eternal. No slumber can seize Him nor sleep. His are all things in the heavens and on earth. Who is there can intercede in His presence except as He permitteth? He knoweth what (appeareth to His creatures as) before or after or behind them. Nor shall they compass aught of His knowledge except as He willeth. His Throne doth extend over the heavens and the earth, and He feeleth no fatigue in guarding and preserving them for He is the Most High, the Supreme (in glory).
[4]O ye who believe! When ye deal with each other, in transactions involving future obligations in a fixed period of time, reduce them to writing Let a scribe write down faithfully as between the parties: let not the scribe refuse to write: as Allah Has taught him, so let him write. Let him who incurs the liability dictate, but let him fear His Lord Allah, and not diminish aught of what he owes. If they party liable is mentally deficient, or weak, or unable Himself to dictate, Let his guardian dictate faithfully, and get two witnesses, out of your own men, and if there are not two men, then a man and two women, such as ye choose, for witnesses, so that if one of them errs, the other can remind her. The witnesses should not refuse when they are called on (For evidence). Disdain not to reduce to writing (your contract) for a future period, whether it be small or big: it is juster in the sight of Allah, More suitable as evidence, and more convenient to prevent doubts among yourselves but if it be a transaction which ye carry out on the spot among yourselves, there is no blame on you if ye reduce it not to writing. But take witness whenever ye make a commercial contract; and let neither scribe nor witness suffer harm. If ye do (such

Qur'an empowers people to act as advocates in resolving disagreements, something that is very relevant today when dealing with matters of "fine print." Allah (swt) commands us to deal with one another with honesty and integrity.

Surah Al Baqarah ends with a beautiful du'a: "Our Lord, do not take us to task if we forget or make mistakes. Our Lord, do not lay upon us a burden such as You had laid upon those before us. Our Lord, do not burden us with more than what we can bear. Pardon us, forgive our sins, and have mercy upon us. You are our Lord, grant us victory over the unbelievers," (2:286). Additionally, Shaytan will not enter the home in which Surah Al Baqarah is recited; also, whoever memorizes and recites the last 10 verses of this surah, Shaytan will not come to them.

Surah Al Baqarah got its title as a result of the story of a man who was killed during the time of Musa (peace be upon him). Musa's people wanted to conceal the transgression because the murderer was well known. When they sought Musa's assistance to settle the matter, Allah instructed them to slaughter a cow. The dialogue that took place between Musa and his people shows that humans complicate matters to the point of making the details of the law more important than the action itself. They tried to avoid the law and the sacrificing of the cow by arguing about the details—its size, color, and shape. As we take this month and review the beauty of the Qur'an, we must recognize the proper methods of implementing the laws of Islam into our lives, but we must not allow the details to overshadow our desire to understand the purpose behind the rulings.

---

harm), it would be wickedness in you. So fear Allah. For it is God that teaches you. And Allah is well acquainted with all things.

Exercises for Surah Al Baqarah

1. Be kind and considerate when interacting with people of other faiths. If they ever encroach on your rights, maintain the best character, the character of the Prophet Muhammad (peace be upon him).

2. Respect the boundaries of contracts that you hold with people. You can practice this even when driving. You agree to a certain set of rules when you obtain your license. Each time you drive remember that is a contract and do your part to not transgress any rules of this contract.

3. When you are afflicted with difficulty. Remind yourself of the verse in this surah in which Allah (swt) promises us that He will never test you with more than you are capable of handling. When you feel overwhelmed, help yourself cope with the du'a in verse 286.

4. In every act you do, connect the letter of the law with the spirit of the law. When you pray five times a day, contemplate the benefits and the reward of stopping for a few minutes for the purpose of remembering your Creator. Be kind to your families and contemplate the benefits and the rewards of doing so. By connecting all aspects of your life to Allah you will appreciate each act of worship and each act of obedience more and it will become easier to do.

Surah Al Imran (3)

The third surah is a Madinan surah, titled Al Imran, or "the family of Imran." "Allah did choose Adam, Nuh, the family of Ibrahim and the family of Imran above all people." Al Imran is similar to Surah Al Baqarah as it makes special reference to the People of the Book as well as discussing the births of Maryam (Mary, the mother of Jesus) and of 'Isa (Jesus, peace be upon him). It shows the belief of Muslims in Maryam and 'Isa and how

24

Maryam has been chosen to be the best of the women of the world. Muslims believe in all of the Prophets from Adam to Muhammad (peace be upon them).

The beauty of this surah is the description of Maryam. The Prophet (peace be upon him) described Maryam as one of the leading women of Paradise. Muslims should appreciate this common belief that we share with Christians. Surah Al Imran also addresses the lessons that resulted from the Battles of Badr and Uhud. This Surah was revealed in four parts: verses 1-32 were revealed shortly after the Battle of Badr (in the second year of the Hijri calendar), followed by verses 64-120. Verses 121 to 200 were received a few years later after the Battle of Uhud. This was then followed a few years later by the final piece, verses 33-63.

Muslims were successful in the Battle of Badr, but when Surah Al Imran was revealed, shortly after the battle, much of the same tensions between the faiths remained. On the occasion of the Battle of Uhud, some of the People of the Book compromised their fundamental principles of faith to join with the idolaters against the Muslims in Madinah. These actions continued after the Battle of Uhud as well. The situation had become so tense that the Companions slept in their armor during this period and stood guard at night in case of sudden attacks.

Muslims of Madinah were required to exercise a great deal of patience, determination, and endurance through this period. Al Imran was revealed during a time of threats, attacks, and violation of the established treaties. The surah reminds Muslims that the Qur'an is not a contradiction of the previous revelations, but rather a confirmation of them. Musa, 'Isa and Muhammad have not called their people to different paths but to the same path.

Allah warns us that excessive wealth and power can

easily lead individuals and nations away from Allah. He repeats this many times in Surah Al Imran, the first mention being verse 10: "Those who reject Faith, neither their possessions nor their progeny will avail them aught against Allah; they are themselves but fuel for the Fire." This verse is very relevant to Muslims today. As we go through these times of financial tests, we must evaluate if our focus is *only* on obtaining worldly possession, or are our actions based on our desire to strive for nearness to Allah Almighty? Wealth and power cannot be used to obtain paradise. We should celebrate the blessings that He has bestowed upon us with gratitude and by using them as a vehicle towards attaining His pleasure.

It was to endorse the Qur'an as a confirmation of the faiths before Islam, that Allah (swt) revealed verse 25: "What will they do when We gather them all together upon a day in which there is no doubt, when every soul will be given what it earned with no injustice whatsoever?" Allah (swt) makes it clear, with this verse and many others throughout the Qur'an, that no person or group of people is better than the other, except in good works and behavior. Why then do we as Muslims see a person as more or less than what they are simply because of their race, ethnicity, social status, means, or any other quality? Since Allah has honored us with another Ramadan, we must strive to overcome the injustices we commit amongst ourselves. If we actively open our hearts and make an effort to befriend someone who we believe to be of different status than us, the result will only be a strengthened brotherhood and nearness to the Creator of *all* of mankind.

Verses 70 and 71 of Surah Al Imran indicate that Allah (swt) is holding people responsible for following the guidance in His book: "People of the Book! Why do you deny Allah's revelations when you are witnesses to their veracity? Why do you confound the true with the false and hide the truth knowingly?' Say: 'We believe in Allah, and in what has been revealed to us and what was revealed to Ibrahim, Isma'il,

Ishaaq, Yaqub, and the Tribes, and in (the Books) given to Musa, 'Isa, and the Prophets, from their Lord: We make no distinction between one and another among them, and to Allahdo we bow our will (in Islam)" This verse shows the emphasis that the Qur'an places on the unity of the Message. Muslims feel attachment to all of the Prophets of Allah, as they are all a part of the Islamic heritage. They came with one message, the message of peace.

Ramadan is a time of reflection and also a time for sacrifice. In verse 93, Allah says: "By no means shall ye attain righteousness unless you give freely of that which you love; and whatever you give, of the truth Allah knoweth it well." In Ramadan, we sacrifice our food, drink, wealth, and time to gain Allah's pleasure and to strive towards righteousness, but the test of giving requires that we ask ourselves, "Are we giving of the things that we love?" The poor and the needy are not people in far off lands. There are many amongst us even in such a prosperous and affluent community. If we give them, are we giving the best of what we have or are we only sacrificing the leftovers that we no longer desire? As we share with others this month, we must remember that attaining Allah's pleasure comes by sacrificing those things that are not always the easiest to separate from ourselves. May Allah open our hearts to giving others what He has given to us and may He help us to remember that no believer loses out by sacrificing in His name.

Surah Al Imran also discusses the prohibition of usury in Islam. Usury, riba, is an issue that Muslim communities often do not like to discuss. However, it is extremely important to discuss our relationship with it, as it is very prevalent today. We have witnessed the damage it has caused in today's economy. People are spending money that they do not have and then are not able to come out of debt. As Muslims, Allah has prohibited us from usury and protected us from the difficult situation it can cause a person to find themselves in. As Muslims we need to avoid spending money that we do not have.

Verses 113-115 remind us that the People of the Book share many of the same principles.[5] Therefore, as Muslims in America, we have to join hands with people of other faiths in enjoining what is right and fighting what is evil. We cannot divide ourselves based on having different faiths. Choosing to be a part of something or to distance from something should be based on working toward the betterment of humanity. We can join together in common causes such as fighting domestic violence, feeding the needy, raising awareness of Autism, providing health care for those in need, and standing up for human rights and justice for all people.

Verses 102-105 cover the topic of the importance of unity of the Muslims.[6] As a community, all of us strive to connect to Allah and believe that division among ourselves weakens our community. Allah (swt) brought people of Arabia from various backgrounds together under the banner of Islam, even though pre-Islamic Arabia was known as a land of war. Today, Muslims must look back to that example and learn from the early Muslims and how the Qur'an served as a tool for unifying people. We should be the example for the rest of the

---

[5]Not all of them are alike: Of the People of the Book are a portion that stand (For the right): They rehearse the Signs of Allah all night long, and they prostrate themselves in adoration.
They believe in Allah and the Last Day; they enjoin what is right, and forbid what is wrong; and they hasten (in emulation) in (all) good works: They are in the ranks of the righteous.
Of the good that they do, nothing will be rejected of them; for Allah knoweth well those that do right.
[6]O ye who believe! Fear Allah as He should be feared, and die not except in a state of Islam.
And hold fast, all together, by the rope which Allah (stretches out for you), and be not divided among yourselves; and remember with gratitude Allah's favour on you; for ye were enemies and He joined your hearts in love, so that by His Grace, ye became brethren; and ye were on the brink of the pit of Fire, and He saved you from it. Thus doth Allah make His Signs clear to you: That ye may be guided. Let there arise out of you a band of people inviting to all that is good, enjoining what is right, and forbidding what is wrong: They are the ones to attain felicity. Be not like those who are divided amongst themselves and fall into disputations after receiving Clear Signs: For them is a dreadful penalty

world, inviting people to peace, to what is right, and to fighting injustice against *any* people. We must not only be the example of good but we must be proactive in calling people to good. Sadly, we still see fighting and loss of life amongst Muslims while the Qur'an is clearly calling us to respect each other and unite in good works. Brotherhood is a blessing from Allah: having people build a connection to each other based on faith and belief in Him. This is a unique and powerful relationship.

The month of Ramadan should teach us to control our anger. Prophet Muhammad (peace be upon him) said a person should respond to another person with whom he is having difficulty by saying, "I am fasting. I am fasting," and avoid cursing or putting down others. Verse 133 encourages us to compete with each other in seeking forgiveness.[7] This is very relevant in this month of Ramadan, in which one third of the month is dedicated to seeking forgiveness from Allah (swt) and drawing nearer to Him. Verse 135 explains how we must also make sure to seek forgiveness from people who we may have wronged or hurt in anyway.[8] It is not acceptable for a servant of Allah to mistreat another servant. Allah shows us mercy and kindness and we must practice these characteristics with those around us.

Usury, whims, desires, loss, anger, and even forgiveness, and our struggle toward what is good: these are all tests from Allah. To break away from what Shaytan whispers to us and to strive to do what Allah has commanded takes deep conviction from the believer. In verse 186, Allah says that we will be tested in our lives by loss of wealth and life, but all of this is just a test. At the same time, He takes us on a journey through the universe

---

[7] Be quick in the race for forgiveness from your Lord, and for a Garden whose width is that (of the whole) of the heavens and of the earth, prepared for the righteous

[8] And those who, having done something to be ashamed of, or wronged their own souls, earnestly bring Allah to mind, and ask for forgiveness for their sins,- and who can forgive sins except Allah.- and are never obstinate in persisting knowingly in (the wrong) they have done.

and the greatness of the universe. We are just a tiny part of it, only a tiny speck in the great and vast universe, yet Allah hears the du'a of each of His servants. May Allah help us to do what He has commanded and to turn away from what He has forbidden.

Exercises for Surah Al Imran

1. Remember how Allah (swt) has honored Maryam and described her as the best of women. Reflect on what you do as an individual to honor the women in your home *and* in your community? Men, look at the women around you and make sure you are supporting and protecting their rights and their honor, not taking advantage of them.
2. Remove usury from your life. Do not purchase things you do not have the money to buy.
3. Actively participate in activities in your community that promote human rights and justice with people across all faiths.
4. When you witness people speaking or acting harshly towards Islam come back to this surah and reread the verses related to the Prophet Muhammad's (peace be upon him) interactions with others in one of the most challenging times in Islamic history.

Surah An Nisa (4)

Surah An Nisa is a Medinan surah that deals with the social problems of Pre-Islamic Arabia. Next to Surah Al Baqarah, it is the longest surah of the Qur'an. It has two elements in it: unity and equality. Both are discussed at the beginning of the surah; the remainder of the surah details the different aspects of these two points. The surah describes the appropriate management of wealth, distribution of inheritance, marriage, method of caring for the women and the orphan, and family rights in general (specifically concerning women and the rights of women). The Qur'an addresses the wrongs in society and the injustice committed against each other, especially in gender equality.

Surah An Nisa was revealed around the time of Surah Al Mumtahanah and Surah Al Ahzab, both of which address the matter of women in Islam. This surah was revealed to the Prophet Muhammad (peace be upon him) to address the lack of appropriate care of women by the Jahiliya Arabs. Women were not treated as equals; these verses brought to the front the rights of women individually, within the family, and within society. Unfortunately, some people use these verses to try to justify limiting the status and rights of the women. The Qur'an protects the vulnerability of women, and of the orphans (in terms of their wealth).

Surah An Nisa discusses the importance of marriage and how it is a covenant between two people. In Surah Al Baqarah, we read about the importance of a covenant and honoring an agreement made between two parties. Unfortunately, nowadays, people take this covenant lightly and think it is something that is disposable, and disregard the potential consequences that dishonoring a contract would have on the greater community. They do not see it as a lifetime commitment that requires hard work and patience.

Verses 22-34 explain whom and how to marry. It explains the obligation of paying the dowry—something that is her right—and doing so without giving any false promise about the intended mahar. The husband is required to provide the mahar to the wife with a good and truthful heart.

Verse 34 is a verse that is often taken out of context.[9] People try to use it to justify acts of abuse in spousal

---

[9] Men are the protectors and maintainers of women, because Allah has given the one more (strength) than the other, and because they support them from their means. Therefore the righteous women are

31

relationships. Their arguments hold no value as we know that the Prophet Muhammad (peace be upon him) never hit anyone—be it man, woman, or child— in his life, with the exception of combat with men on the field of battle. It is prohibited for Muslims to engage in combat with women and children or to attack them. If placed in its true context, we see that the verse appoints men as protectors of women. Keeping in mind the context in which the Qur'an was revealed, this was an elevation in the status of women. It is one of the many verses that countered the pre-Islamic belief that women were property and instead assigned men to be caretakers of their safety, reputation, and needs. The verse says that men are "qawamun," coming from the word, qayim and qayim means to take care of someone.

Another reason that the verses of this surah are at times abused is because of the number of times that it addresses men. When talking about the rights of women, Allah (swt) is addressing the men out of His infinite wisdom, understanding that men often transgress the boundaries by use of power, so He, the All Knowing, addresses them directly. This is done in a similar manner in the first verse immediately telling the believers to acknowledge the greatness of Allah, His ability to create humanity from two people from a single soul, and that He is ever watchful of all things. He uses strong descriptions to emphasize the extreme seriousness of the matters laid out in the surah.

In wealth and inheritance, Surah An Nisa organizes the matter of finances for the Muslims to avoid dispute between them. As has been stated, the Qur'an talks about protection of women's rights; Surah An Nisa specifically mentions treating

---

devoutly obedient, and guard in (the husband's) absence what Allah would have them guard. As to those women on whose part ye fear disloyalty and ill-conduct, admonish them (first), (Next), refuse to share their beds, (And last) strike them (lightly); but if they return to obedience, seek not against them Means (of annoyance): For Allah is Most High, great (above you all).

them with kindness and calls men to fulfill their role in being protectors of the rights of women and be just and fair with them. It also covers the matter of their inheritance—something they were previously denied. People of the pre-Islamic era used to give inheritance to the males but denied it to the females. Allah commanded that both take a share. In the situation where the brother is given twice the amount of the sister(s), it is because the portion given to the brother is not only allocated for him, but for care of his sister(s) as well.

The Surah also protects another vulnerable group: the orphans. Allah commands that the property of the orphan be protected until they reach adulthood, at which time the property should be given to the orphan himself. The quality of the property should not be compromised to increase the caretaker's possessions through the orphan's property, as that is a weighty sin. It is clear through these verses that Allah is demanding that His servants be people of justice. In verse 135, He emphasizes this by explaining that we should stand against injustice wherever it occurs, *even* if within our own families. [10]

Allah (swt) addresses those who question His decree regarding the care of the women and the orphans. He explains the importance of obeying Allah (swt) and His messenger and that no one, with true faith and belief in Allah Almighty, will question His command. Faith is tested with highs and lows every day. Allah reminds us in verse 101 that even in the most difficult times we must never give up on our prayer and never stray from our good deeds.[11] This is our connection with Allah and it is through prayer and good works that we attain that level of obedience without questioning.

---

[10]O ye who believe! stand out firmly for justice, as witnesses to Allah, even as against yourselves, or your parents, or your kin, and whether it be (against) rich or poor: for Allah can best protect both. Follow not the lusts (of your hearts), lest ye swerve, and if ye distort (justice) or decline to do justice, verily Allah is well- acquainted with all that ye do.
[11]When ye travel through the earth, there is no blame on you if ye shorten your prayers, for fear the Unbelievers May attack you: For the Unbelievers are unto you open enemies.

The later verses deal with the issue of inheritance and the importance of maintaining ties of kinship. The ties of relations are not cut off at death; rather, they guide the distribution of wealth in order to prevent it from remaining in the hands of one individual. This eliminates dispute after the death of a loved one. Surah An Nisa, beginning to end, is considered clear guidance and instructions on how to live our lives on a personal, community, and global level.

Exercises for Surah AnNisa

1. If you do not have one, write your will today.
2. If you are single, learn the details of a marriage contract. If you are married, find a lawyer who can provide you with a Shariah compliant example and compare it to your marriage contract.
3. If a dispute arises between you and another person, seek arbitration. This is particularly important in marital and familial disputes.
4. Identify situations or times that you have not been just to a creation of Allah. Write each one down. Then write down the steps you will take to correct the injustice or to make sure it is not repeated.
5. Identify and commit to one act you can do on a regular basis to protect the rights of orphans in your community or around the world.

Surah Al Maidah (5)

Al Maidah is a surah known by two titles: Al Maidah, meaning "table," and Al Uqud, meaning "the covenants." Al Uqud indicates the surah's many subjects while Al Maidah comes from 'Isa's (peace be upon him) supplication to Allah for food from heaven. Al Maidah contains some of the final revelations of law that were revealed to the beloved Prophet Muhammad (peace be upon him), as it was one of the final surahs to be revealed.

As this is a surah that makes many references to law, Allah (swt) explains in it the permissibility of consuming land animals and water animals. Here it is explained that the meat of the camel, sheep, and cows is permissible for consumption, as long as they are found alive and slaughtered in the name of Allah. Qatadah, a great scholar of *tafsir*, said, "The meat of the dead animals is like animals slaughtered without Allah's name being pronounced at the time of slaughtering." This defines those animals that are being referred to as prohibited for consumption. This type of animal is considered to be both religiously and physically harmful.

Fish is an exception; it is reported that the Messenger of Allah was asked about seawater. He said, "Its water is pure and its dead are permissible." Allah has demanded mercy and kindness amongst human beings numerous times in the Qur'an. He demands this kindness and mercy be extended even into our interactions with His other creations, even if they are the animals that we eat. Allah has made forbidden to the Muslims the meat of an animal that died by strangulation, violent blows, or beatings. It is necessary to make the process as easy on the animal as possible and out of view of other animals.

Allah (swt) references in this surah, as we have seen in Al Baqarah and Al Imran, the importance of maintaining a covenant. As was discussed in the previous readings, these are covenants that are made between people, but also include the covenants that are made between Allah and His servant. When we are submitting ourselves to Allah, we are agreeing to accept the commands He has sent down. We must remember it is not for us to choose which of His commands we will obey and which we will not.

In this surah, Allah (swt) sends down the command to perform *wudu*, the purification ritual required for prayer. Ibn 'Umar (May Allah be pleased with him) said that the Messenger of Allah said, "Allah does not accept charity from one who commits prayer without purity." *Wudu* is required of the person in a state of impurity and is recommended even in the case of purity, as is mentioning the name of Allah before making *wudu*. *Wudu* is not only a means to ibadah but it is also an act of *ibadah* itself. *Wudu* is a spiritual cleansing. It should be done with concentration and should not be rushed because each motion purifies the believer of his sins. Wudu helps with mental preparation for the salah, the time of direct connection with Allah (swt). In addition, wudu is a means of reducing stress and anger. Rather than engaging in hurtful conversation or using disliked tones or terms, we should make it a habit to use this act of worship when we find ourselves stressed or angry. Our reward, God willing, will be multiplied for removing ourselves from anger and for bringing ourselves closer to Allah through *wudu*.

Surah Al Maidah also shares a story of Prophet 'Isa (may Allah be pleased with him) and the Injil. The Qur'an recognizes the miracles connected to this great Prophet of Allah. He (swt) puts great emphasis on 'Isa being the son of Maryam, (may Allah be pleased with them both). Maryam is Mary in the Biblical tradition. He mentions her name ten times with the name of 'Isa, while no father is mentioned, making it clear there is no biological father for 'Isa. Surah Al Maidah mentions the Holy Spirit, which in the Islamic perspective is a reference to the angel Jibreel. 'Isa was given the ability to speak in the cradle and was granted knowledge and a unique ability to cure people of their illnesses. The Qur'an makes it clear that these are not because 'Isa possessed any attribute of Allah; rather that Allah had blessed him with these unique abilities.

Verse 32 of Surah Al Maidah talks about the value of human life and the severity of unjustly taking life.[12] It relates the

---

[12]On that account: We ordained for the Children of Israel that if any one slew a person - unless it be for murder or for spreading mischief in the land - it would be as if he slew the whole people: and if any one saved a life, it would be as if he saved the life of the whole people.

story of Adam (peace be upon him) and his two children, one taking the life of the other. There were no nations and races at that time, only this family; the removal of one life was a detriment to all of humanity. Today, as Muslims, we need to take a strong stand against those who harm or take innocent life. There is absolutely no justification for such an injustice merely to convey a political message or as collateral damage. Everyone matters because that is a representation of all of humanity. The sanctity of life is universal.

Also mentioned in this surah are references to the prohibition of alcohol, something that can kill a person and permission to eat what is otherwise unlawful in order to protect a person's health. Allah (swt) conveys the value of life in these verses and the flexibility of the law in preservation of life.

Exercises for Surah Al Maidah

1. Be kind to all animals. Look at the source of the meat you eat. If the source is cruel to the animals in their life, or in their death, choose a different source.
2. When you find yourself becoming angry or overwhelmed by stress, make *wudu*.
3. The next time you make *wudu*, take your time. Concentrate on what you are doing and whom you are preparing yourself to stand before. Reflect on the purification process of *wudu*, washing your sins off of you.
4. In today's world there is a great need for protection of human life. Feeding the hungry, assisting the ill or injured, and giving blood are easy ways to do this. Identify ways that you can personally help protect and

Then although there came to them Our apostles with clear signs, yet, even after that, many of them continued to commit excesses in the land.

preserve human life. Identify ways that you can help your community/mosque to do this.

5. Find the callings of Allah in this surah (verses starting with "O ye who believe" or "O you people"). What ways are you going to respond to these direct calls for action?

Surah Al An'am (6)

Surah Al An'am is a Makkan surah and was revealed as a whole, 165 verses long. It is recorded by At Tabarani that Ibn Abbas said, "All of Surah Al An'am was revealed at night, accompanied by 70,000 angels, raising their voices in glorification of Allah." The previous surahs had already covered the discussion of earlier revelations and how the people of those revelations should have adhered to what was sent down to them. It is a sign for us to be mindful of our actions in adhering to the Qur'an. This surah follows those discussions by turning its focus to the situation in which the Arabs found themselves, surrounded by idolaters.

The people of Arabia had forgotten the bounties that Allah had bestowed upon them and, after some time, the worship of idols had become the norm. Allah (swt) reminds mankind of the bounties that He has bestowed upon His creations. In verses 95-99, Allah (swt) explains how He brings forth sustenance for the earth and, in turn, for all of His creations.[13] We should consider how Allah (swt) does not allow

---

[13]It is Allah Who causeth the seed-grain and the date-stone to split and sprout. He causeth the living to issue from the dead, and He is the one to cause the dead to issue from the living. That is Allah. then how are ye deluded away from the truth? He it is that cleaveth the day-break (from the dark): He makes the night for rest and tranquillity, and the sun and moon for the reckoning (of time): Such is the judgment and ordering of (Him), the Exalted in Power, the Omniscient.
It is He Who maketh the stars (as beacons) for you, that ye may guide yourselves, with their help, through the dark spaces of land and sea: We detail Our signs for people who know. It is He Who hath produced you from a single person: here is a place of sojourn and a place of departure: We detail Our signs for people who understand.

the reader of the verse to attribute His description to anything other than Him. Allah (swt) does not say that He brought forth the "vegetation", because one would then attribute it to the seed. Rather, He says He brought forth the seed and caused it to open into vegetation. He doesn't say He sends the sun and the moon as a passing of time which one might then relate back to the rotation of the earth, but Allah states in the verse that it is He who causes the rotation of the earth: "He is the cleaver of the daybreak (from the dark)."

This is something for us to contemplate in each blessing in our lives; what is the very source of that blessing? We are the ones who pick the vegetables and cook the meals and eat our food, but where would we be if Allah (swt) had not caused that seed to split deep within the earth and then sent down the rain from the heavens, causing it to grow?

In verse 122, Allah (swt) clarifies why He asks us to ponder on the splitting of the seed and the breaking of the dawn: "Is he who was dead, and We gave him life, and set for him a light, whereby he can walk among men like he who is in the darkness from which he can never come out? Thus it is made fair seeming to the disbelievers that which they used to do." Here we see the metaphor of a man who believed and a man who had no faith. Before faith and purpose, the former was like a man walking in confusion and darkness but by Allah's Grace, he was given the light that enabled him to see his path. The man who does not have faith walks in spiritual darkness and cannot walk a path without deviating from it. Allah has blessed

---

It is He Who sendeth down rain from the skies: with it We produce vegetation of all kinds: from some We produce green (crops), out of which We produce grain, heaped up (at harvest); out of the date-palm and its sheaths (or spathes) (come) clusters of dates hanging low and near: and (then there are) gardens of grapes, and olives, and pomegranates, each similar (in kind) yet different (in variety): when they begin to bear fruit, feast your eyes with the fruit and the ripeness thereof. Behold! in these things there are signs for people who believe.

us with the light of Islam and we must embrace the blessing and strive to share the light with those around us.

Allah (swt) has used the previous verses to reaffirm the oneness of Allah, the Creator and the Sustainer of the universe and all that is in it. He follows these verses by the peak of the surah, verses 151 and 152, in which He sets forth the laws for mankind.[14] He first prohibits partnering anything with Him and immediately follows this firm and undebatable statement with kindness to parents. Allah (swt) commands us to obey Him and we do so out of both fear and love for Him. Why do so many of us then treat our parents with so little kindness and respect? What makes it okay for a child to disrespect his or her parents? Allah has honored them by placing the command of kind treatment toward parents directly after the command to assign no partner with Him—a command that, if one were to reject this, he or she would be rejecting the faith. He continues the verse by reminding us to distance ourselves from shameful deeds, to protect and preserve life, and to protect the rights and property of the orphans.

In verse 160, Allah (swt) encourages the believers to strive for good work and to follow His commands and obey His law, "Whoever brings a good deed shall have ten times the like thereof to his credit and whoever brings an evil deed shall have only recompense of the like thereof, and they will not be wronged." Allah knows the weakness of human beings and that

---

[14]Say: "Come, I will rehearse what Allah hath (really) prohibited you from": Join not anything as equal with Him; be good to your parents; kill not your children on a plea of want;- We provide sustenance for you and for them;- come not nigh to shameful deeds. Whether open or secret; take not life, which Allah hath made sacred, except by way of justice and law: thus doth He command you, that ye may learn wisdom. And come not nigh to the orphan's property, except to improve it, until he attain the age of full strength; give measure and weight with (full) justice;- no burden do We place on any soul, but that which it can bear;- whenever ye speak, speak justly, even if a near relative is concerned; and fulfil the covenant of Allah. thus doth He command you, that ye may remember.

we all commit sins. But a believer should never lose hope. Out of His generosity, Allah counts each sin as only one sin and Allah has made the weight of each of our good deeds multiplied. As we enjoy this blessed month of Ramadan, we should recognize that none of us is perfect and we all have behaviors or habits that need to be perfected. Allah promised in the verse above that each of our good deeds will be multiplied; but in this blessed month, they will be multiplied to an even greater amount. Let us each choose a deed that we can add to our Ramadan routine that will bring us closer to Allah (swt) and try our best to carry that enhanced routine from this Ramadan until the next.

May Allah forgive us for our sins and help us to always walk in His path.

Exercises for Surah An'am

1. Connect yourself and your family to the source of blessings in your life. Visit a farm in your area and pick your own fruits or vegetables. Identify the source of the food: roots, eggs, bush, and trees.
2. Think about the source of this blessing when you sit down to enjoy it. And, make a commitment to show gratitude for these blessings by being more environmentally conscious.
3. Remind yourselves of Allah's infinite knowledge. Sit in front of a tree in the fall and count every leaf that falls from the tree. Allah has knowledge of every detail of every leaf that falls from every single tree. How does your knowledge of this one tree compare with that of Allah?
4. Evaluate your relationship with your parents. Keep a childhood picture of yourself with your parents somewhere where you are often reminded of it. If one or both of your parents have passed away, pray for

41

them after every prayer. If you have the blessing of your parents still being with you, try to do the following: stop all things that are displeasing to them, honor them by treating them better than anyone else you meet, and give them your time by helping them and by visiting them.

5. Take one day and write down everything that you did that day. Reflect on how your deeds would add up when Allah multiplies your every good deed by ten times. Contemplate on the Mercy of Allah in calculating our deeds.

Surah AlA'raf (7)

Surah Al A'raf is one of the longest of the Makkan surahs. It is the first surah that discusses the lives of the prophets in detail, beginning with Adam (peace be upon him) through the Prophet Muhammad (peace be upon him), including the details of the struggles of Musa (may Allah be pleased with him). The name Al A'raf was taken from the mentioning of a fence between Heaven and Hell. Some say that the word *"A'raf"* itself means "heights." The previous surah, Al An'am discusses the concept of *Tawhid*, the Oneness of Allah, and the history of those before the Prophet Muhammad (peace be upon him). In contrast, Surah Al A'raf discusses human struggles, all of which are blessed with lessons that are still relevant to us today.

Allah (swt) begins Surah Al A'raf with a powerful statement: The Qur'an has been revealed and we should have no doubts or questioning of it. Allah (swt) immediately, at the beginning of this revelation, consoles the Prophet (peace be upon him). He makes known the difficulty that will be faced upon preaching the Book of Allah. He makes it clear that the test has begun and there is no source of help or comfort, except in Him (swt). This is a lesson we must take and remember in each struggle that we face. Whether it is financial, emotional, or spiritual difficulty, we must always remember that it is in Allah alone that we will find comfort and help.

In verse 27, Allah (swt) warns us not to allow Shaytan to take advantage of us in the same way as he tried to take advantage of our father, Adam (peace be upon him).[15] This world is nothing more than a test for mankind. None of us is perfect and while we must always steer away from that which is displeasing to Allah, we will at times commit sin. Allah (swt) calls the believers to strive toward repentance. He reminds us of the story of Adam and his removal from Paradise, but that Adam (peace be upon him) still sought forgiveness and Allah granted him what he asked. This is a message to us that despite what may be sitting on our scales, the doors of forgiveness are always unlocked. Allah (swt) is only waiting for us to knock on them. Similarly, Allah (swt) emphasizes the importance of forgiving others who may cause us distress or hurt. Fostering hatred and anger are destructive to the spiritual self and in turn damaging to our relationships with Allah (swt). We must try to forgive each other, as Allah is always forgiving with us.

However, there are those who—as described in verses 175 and 176—are shown the signs of Allah but choose to disregard them.[16] They have seen the guidance but choose to turn away from it. An appropriate parable is of men who possess great skills and positions and are blessed with the opportunities of

---

[15] O ye Children of Adam! Let not Satan seduce you, in the same manner as He got your parents out of the Garden, stripping them of their raiment, to expose their shame: for he and his tribe watch you from a position where ye cannot see them: We made the evil ones friends (only) to those without faith.

[16] Relate to them the story of the man to whom We sent Our signs, but he passed them by: so Satan followed him up, and he went astray. If it had been Our will, We should have elevated him with Our signs; but he inclined to the earth, and followed his own vain desires. His similitude is that of a dog: if you attack him, he lolls out his tongue, or if you leave him alone, he (still) lolls out his tongue. That is the similitude of those who reject Our signs; So relate the story; perchance they may reflect.

spiritual comprehension but they turn away. This is like a person who frees himself from his garment which guards him against harmful matters, and exposes himself to Shaytan and his calling.

As we benefit from the many fruits that Ramadan has to offer, by fasting and engaging in extra *ibadah* and *dhikr*, we are sewing a stronger garment to shield ourselves from the evils of Shaytan. Ramadan is a month of training; it is a time to bring the Nafs back to focusing on Allah (swt), to control habits, and to learn the virtue of refraining from indulgence, especially at the expense of our spiritual well being. The only thing that keeps us spiritually alive is our connection to Allah, so we must work hard to preserve that connection. The spiritual upliftment we feel in Ramadan should be maintained by continuous *ibadah* and *dhikr* throughout the year. Therefore, we should not shed this garment after Ramadan has passed, as we will only expose ourselves to the accursed Shaytan.

While Ramadan teaches us to focus on Allah, He (swt) reminds us in verse 33 that we may also enjoy what He has provided us in this life.[17] However, we must do so with mindfulness and balance. If we enjoy what is good in this life, Allah will give us the same in the next life with greater enjoyment. If we enjoy what is decreed as evil or impermissible, the enjoyment is only in this short life and the recompense will be seen in the life to come.

The end of Surah Al A'raf also contains the first Sajdah at-Tilawah in the Qur'an. *Sajdah at-Tilawah* is only one sajdah. While there are multiple supplications that can be made, this one may be easy for those who are still learning: "O Allah, record for me a reward for this (prostration), and remove from

---

[17]Say: the things that my Lord hath indeed forbidden are: shameful deeds, whether open or secret; sins and trespasses against truth or reason; assigning of partners to Allah, for which He hath given no authority; and saying things about Allah of which ye have no knowledge.

me a sin. Save it for me and accept it from me just as You had accepted it from Your servant Dawud." To this act of worship, which is repeated only fifteen times in the Qur'an, Shaytan responds with the following cry: "'O woe, he was ordered to prostrate and he did, so for him or her is Paradise? I was ordered to prostrate and I disobeyed, so for me is Hell.'"

May Allah protect us from engaging in what displeases Him. May He protect us from Shaytan and his whispers and may He make us of the people of Paradise.

Exercises for Surah Al A'raf

---

1. When faced with difficulty, go to a quiet place. Talk to Allah (swt) about your difficulty and seek help from Him. Make this du'a: "O Allah, there is no ease except in that which You have made easy, and You make the difficult, if You wish, easy."

2. In Ramadan we evaluate the level of influence Shaytan has on us. Identify the ways Shaytan tricks you into wrongdoing. Now establish a plan, step by step, of what you will do to overcome them.

3. Allah has warned us against arrogance in verse 146. Evaluate the role of culture in making decisions in your life. Are your decisions determined by the word of Allah or by your cultural background even when contradictory to the word of Allah? Evaluate how much culture and ego influence obedience to Allah.

4. Learn one of these two du'as to be said during *Sajdah At Tilawah*:
   a. "O Allah, record for me a reward for this (prostration), and remove from me a sin. Save it for me and accept it from me just as You have accepted it from Your servant Dawud."
   b. "My face fell prostrate before He created it and brought fourth its faculties of hearing and

seeing by His might and power. So Blessed is Allah the best of Creators."

Surah Al Anfal (8)

Surah Al Anfal discusses historical events, such as major battles. The Quraysh severely oppressed the Muslims and denied them freedom of religion and freedom of assembly. Before the battle, the Prophet prayed for a peaceful solution so there would be no violence. This surah talks about the comfort and the victory that Allah (swt) gives to those who strive in His cause. The Prophet (peace be upon him) and his companions were often confronted with many difficult situations. Their property and wealth were seized and they were often under threat of attack. In battle, the Prophet and the companions were outnumbered by three times as many of the opposing forces, yet Allah (swt) granted them victory. The Muslim soldiers no doubt felt concern upon learning of the number of enemies they would have to face, but they placed their trust in Allah knowing that failure would only find them if they turned away from Him. From this we learn that victory and success for the believers are not necessarily found in numbers or in power, but in devotion and sincerity to Allah (swt).

This lesson takes Muslims onto the field of battle that is within the *Nafs*, soul. As we have read in the previous surah, Allah is calling us to use Ramadan as a time of training for our souls, a preparation for the months we will face before next Ramadan. Unfortunately, we often find Muslim in non-Muslim environments being neglectful of their obligatory worship because they are afraid of what their coworkers or peers will think of them. It is natural for people to feel, at times, that they are 'out of place' as they are doing something that may be outside of the norm of the environment around them.

However, this becomes a problem when the feelings lead a person to be neglectful of Allah, the One who has created us and granted us the ability and health to live our lives. Allah (swt) is reminding us that, if we sincerely work towards establishing our faith within our hearts and devote ourselves to constant improvement in our relationship with Him, He will make the path smooth and easy to that which we are striving for. Allah (swt) explains in a *Hadith Qudsi* that there is nothing more beloved to Him than His servant engaging in acts that He has commanded for them. With each extra effort and struggle, Allah's love for His servant only increases. This hadith also reflects Allah's willingness to bridge any gap between His servant and Himself, as long as we desire to be closer to Him.

This surah reminds us of the great tests that the first generation of Muslims faced. Muslims were physically and emotionally tortured in Makkah to the point that they had to flee in order to protect their lives. They were abandoned by their families and left with nothing. The Makkans took away their wealth, limiting their means for protection and defense. Muslims were under constant difficulty and hardship, but their faith remained strong and hearts remained centered on Allah (swt) and the attainment of Paradise. We should look back at the struggles of such people each day and be grateful for their courage and perseverance. The current state, in which Muslims find themselves, easily able to practice Islam in a land so far from Makkah, is a direct result of the efforts of those who have gone before. We must appreciate what they have built for us and strive to further improve the state of Muslims in our own masjid, community, country, and around the world. At the same time, it should be recognized that each of us has our own trials that should not be taken lightly. Every person's test is his or her own, and every test is an opportunity to draw us nearer to Allah (swt). We must evaluate each situation and determine what would be pleasing to Him. May Allah establish *Iman*, or faith, in our hearts, and help us to come closer to Him through our trials and to not allow ourselves to distance ourselves from Him.

Exercises for Surah Al Anfal

1. Incorporate the stories of the Prophets of Allah into your life. Take notes when reading their stories from the Qur'an. Write down the areas in which their stories relate to your current situation and how can you replicate the responses they offered?

2. Take steps to learn the history of Islam, the Qur'an, and the Prophets of Allah. Plan to join a class, or read books focusing on their history of the prophets.

3. Even after 13 years of intense oppression, the Qur'an did not ask for physical confrontation with the oppressors. Identify rational and peaceful methods that you, as an individual or as a family, can employ to cope with the discomfort that today's issues of injustice cause.

4. Remember that unity does not mean uniformity. Spend a few days to a week writing down the things you did each day and what you set as priorities throughout those days. Evaluate if you compromised any commands or values in an effort to conform to the environment around you or if you were able to fulfill your requirements regardless. If you are in the first category, reevaluate if the environment that causes you to compromise is worth staying in and how can you adjust things in such a way that you no longer compromise commands of values.

4

Surah At Tawbah to Surah Al 'Isra

Surah At Tawbah (9)

Surah At Tawbah gets its name from the many verses it contains that emphasize the nature and conditions of repentance. It is also called Al-Bara'a, "release," taken from the first word in the surah. A third name for this surah is Al-Fadiha, or "exposure." While Surah At Tawbah is unique in many ways, the first and most obvious distinction from other surahs is that it does not begin with the Basmallah. There is no other surah in the Qur'an with this characteristic. Scholars say this is a result of the urgency of these verses. Surah At Tawbah is a Madinan surah, the beginning of which was revealed after the Battle of Tabuk. That year, Abu Bakr (may Allah be pleased with him) served as the leader for Hajj. Ali (may Allah be pleased with him) later followed to convey Surah Bara'a to the Makkans, a declaration of the ending of the Jahiliya—the pre-Islamic era, "Age of Ignorance" period. It was one of the last surahs revealed to the beloved Prophet (peace be upon him). Surah At Tawbah is a continuation of the end of Surah Al Anfal, discussing treaties. Surah At Tawbah concludes the "seven long surahs."

This ninth surah of the Qur'an covers the phenomenon of hypocrisy and the characters of the hypocrites, such as staying behind in times of battle, withholding money from those in need, mocking those who give, and the erecting of Masjid Dirar in order to gather believers and then cause division between them. But Allah (swt) exposes the hypocrites and reminds the believers not to become anxious, that indeed Allah is aware of all of the plans of the hypocrites and He is aware of all that transpires. He ordered the Prophet to destroy Masjid Dirar (the Arabic word *Dirar* means "to cause harm") built by the hypocrites. It is from stories such as these that Allah makes it clear that, though people may try to bring division or cause destruction in the name of religion, they will not succeed as there is no place for it in Islam.

Verse 18 discusses the importance of taking care of mosques, as well as the characteristics of people who help to establish them.[18] Today, as a community, we have to work to maintain our institutions and mosques. A masjid (mosque) is a place where a person should feel a sense of community and a sense of love, and environment of brotherhood and sisterhood.

Surah At Tawbah also mentions the behaviors of human beings in regards to accepting the order of Allah. Allah (swt) recognizes the laziness of the human beings in responding to His call. Allah mentions the habit of holding back and not spending for His sake, especially in the matter of *Zakah*, almsgiving. This is covered in verses 34 and 35.[19] While we know that Allah is never in need of our obedience, He reminds us of those who need us to execute His command. In verse 60, Allah (swt) lays down the categories of those worthy of Zakah.[20] They are our brothers and sisters who need us to stand up and fulfill our responsibilities by giving them what is already rightfully theirs.

---

[18]The mosques of Allah shall be visited and maintained by such as believe in Allah and the Last Day, establish regular prayers, and practise regular charity, and fear none (at all) except Allah. It is they who are expected to be on true guidance.

[19]O ye who believe! there are indeed many among the priests and anchorites, who in Falsehood devour the substance of men and hinder (them) from the way of Allah. And there are those who bury gold and silver and spend it not in the way of Allah. announce unto them a most grievous penalty-

On the Day when heat will be produced out of that (wealth) in the fire of Hell, and with it will be branded their foreheads, their flanks, and their backs.- "This is the (treasure) which ye buried for yourselves: taste ye, then, the (treasures) ye buried!"

[20]Alms are for the poor and the needy, and those employed to administer the (funds); for those whose hearts have been (recently) reconciled (to Truth); for those in bondage and in debt; in the cause of Allah. and for the wayfarer: (thus is it) ordained by Allah, and Allah is full of knowledge and wisdom.

We must remember that these are not people in distant parts of the world, but brothers and sisters who walk the halls of the very mosques that we do. Who are we to deny them what Allah has already made theirs?

Oftentimes, people are hesitant to part with material things, like money, because of the effort that was put forth to earn it. Allah (swt) reminds us in verses 75 and 76 that, while effort on our part is a means to obtaining wealth, the source is Allah.[21] The believers are reminded in times of difficulty that we often seek Allah's assistance and promise to use what blessings He provides us in His way. However, when He provides, we turn our backs and forget the promises that were made. Unfortunately, this stems from people failing to put their full trust in Allah (swt). In verse 40, Allah (swt) reminds us that we must have unshakable belief in Allah and His Messenger.[22] He reminds us of the story of Prophet Muhammad (peace be upon him) and Abu Bakr (may Allah be pleased with him) as they fled from being captured by the Makkans. Abu Bakr (may Allah be pleased with him) turned to the Prophet of Allah, while hiding in the cave, and said, "O Rasul Allah, those people are at the door of the cave. If one were to look down, they would see us." The Prophet responded, "O Abu Bakr, what do you think about two people, and Allah is the third?" The lesson is that, if we are striving in the way of Allah and put our trust in Him, we do not have to fear anything or despair, for we are in the company of Allah (swt). This concept of being in Allah's presence through

---

[21]Amongst them are men who made a covenant with Allah, that if He bestowed on them of His bounty, they would give (largely) in charity, and be truly amongst those who are righteous. But when He did bestow of His bounty, they became covetous, and turned back (from their covenant), averse (from its fulfilment).

[22]If ye help not (your leader), (it is no matter): for Allah did indeed help him, when the Unbelievers drove him out: he had no more than one companion; they two were in the cave, and he said to his companion, "Have no fear, for Allah is with us": then Allah sent down His peace upon him, and strengthened him with forces which ye saw not, and humbled to the depths the word of the Unbelievers. But the word of Allah is exalted to the heights: for Allah is Exalted in might, Wise.

striving for what He has commanded is an extremely important and relevant concept for Muslims today. It reminds us that so long as we have Allah on our side, nothing else matters. If we work hard to stay close to Him in good times then in times of difficulty or hardship, Allah will be our source of comfort and ease.

Sacrificing in the way of Allah(swt) is probably most relevant to us now in this month of Ramadan. Many of us give more of our time and wealth during this month, as we are encouraged to do. Some may be able to do more than others. In verse 79, Allah (swt) emphasizes the importance of never belittling the deeds or efforts of another person.[23] He forbids mockery of another person's actions. The Prophet Muhammad (peace be upon him) made every effort to unify the Muslims into a strong *Ummah*, supportive of each other. It is important for us to follow that example and to appreciate every effort that a person makes. Allah (swt) judges on the quality of the intention, we should not then make it our place to judge on the quantity of something material or worldly. A person's twenty five cents may outweigh twenty-five dollars if the intention of the former is more pure than that of the latter, so leave the judgment to Allah.

Allah (swt) concludes this surah with a beautiful *dua'*, supplication or prayer. When we say this du'a, Allah will bring us comfort and ease: "Allah sufficeth me: There is no God but He: On Him is my trust—He the Lord of the Throne (of Glory) Supreme," (9:129).

---

[23]Those who slander such of the believers as give themselves freely to (deeds of) charity, as well as such as can find nothing to give except the fruits of their labour,- and throw ridicule on them,- Allah will throw back their ridicule on them: and they shall have a grievous penalty.

Exercises for Surah At Tawbah

---

1. Seeking repentance is not a passive act. Do not sit and wait for Allah to forgive you, make extra effort to seek it. Identify ways that you can express greater sincerity in seeking forgiveness. Some suggestions are: sit a little longer after prayer than you do on an average day and make *istighfar*; sacrifice something of yours for someone else, do something purely to make someone happy for the sake of Allah; most importantly, remove any sin from your life.
2. Giving charity is also something that requires an active effort. It is not the responsibility of the poor person to come to you and ask. Go out and seek those in need, through the masjid or the larger community and share your blessings with them.
3. Never hold back your charity because it feels insufficient. Remember Allah has the power to multiply it infinitely. He (swt) only asks you to give with sincerity.
4. Rely on Allah. If you feel afraid of what the future holds for you, read verse 51, "Say: 'Nothing will happen to us except what Allah has decreed for us: He is our Protector: and on Allah let the Believers put their trust.'"

Surah Yunus (10)

Surah Yunus is a Makkan surah that discusses the various aspects of *aqidah* (creed). Yunus is Jonah in the Bible. This surah refers back to previous revelations but emphasizes the Qur'an as the final revelation. The surah begins by describing the message and the Messenger and draws the connection between these two. It expresses how the Prophet is a reflection of the Qur'an as he manifested it in all aspects of his life. At the same time, the Qur'an talks about the relationship of the Creator with His creations, but emphasizes the impossibility of any of His creations having the divinity of Allah, as Allah is One, Alone.

The second topic covered is the actions of the rejecters of the message. They accused the Prophet of fabricating the Qur'an and they spread rumors about him being nothing more than a poet. Allah challenges those that mocked the Prophet and tells them to produce something similar to the like of the Qur'an. None of them was able to do this. It is one of the great miracles of the Qur'an that the non-Muslim Arabs recognized the superiority of the language and were unable to duplicate it. The Qur'an differentiated itself from *Diwan* (compilation of poetry) from its very beginning. In Arabic poetry, a line is called *"bayt,"* while in the Qur'an it is an *"ayah."* The end of a *bayt* is *"qafiyah,"* and the end of an *ayah* is *"fasilah."* Similarly, a collection of verses in poetry is a *"qasida,"* while in the Qur'an it is a *"surah."* Allah (swt) uses these different terms to completely separate the revelation from an Arabian pastime.

The language of the Qur'an is only one of its many miracles. It was compiled over the span of 23 years and addressed a wide range of topics, never once contradicting itself. The style and language of the Qur'an is so unique that it was impossible for the Prophet to have learned it from a teacher of Arabic as there was no one who had spoken in the same manner as the Qur'an. These facts in themselves are proof that no one could fabricate such a text.

Though Prophet Yunus was only mentioned once, in verse 98, Surah Yunus takes its name from the description it gives of Prophet Yunus (may Allah be pleased with him). He was a prophet whom Allah had sent to the people of the area of Iraq. He called people to believe in the One Allah, but they continuously rejected him. Yunus lost hope in changing his people. Without the permission of Allah, Prophet Yunus decided to leave; but the Will of Allah prevails over all things, and Allah stopped Prophet Yunus by capturing him in the stomach of a whale. He (swt) made the prophets like us in many ways. We must look to their stories and realize that they are not so different from us and that we can benefit from the lessons that came out their trials, sorrows, errors and successes. Surah Yunus is a great reminder of this fact. Allah does not relinquish His prophet for abandoning his people. Even the Prophets of Allah stood to be corrected. We must not give up on ourselves for doing the same from time to time. But we should remember that Prophet Yunus confronted this difficult time and his mistake by turning to Allah with one of the most beautiful du'as: And remember *Dhun-nun*, when he departed in wrath: He imagined that Allah had no power over him! But he cried through the depths of darkness, "There is no god but Thou: glory to Thee: I was indeed wrong!" (21:87). Is there any situation we have faced comparable to being swallowed and sitting in the stomach of a whale?

In verse 107, Allah explains that He is the one who has complete control over all that happens in the universe, and that no good or harm will come to a person without His Will.[24] Yunus (may Allah be pleased with Him) was in the stomach of a whale—who else could return him safely to his people after he faced certain death? We must always remember to turn to Allah (swt) and put our trust in Him, even in the most difficult of times.

Prophet Yunus recognized the severity of his mistake and the truth of his mission. He returned to the same people who had rejected him time and time again, and they returned to their Creator and believed in the message he delivered. In verse 99, Allah reminds us through this beautiful story that Allah alone is the one who guides people and He has not placed any difficulty in His religion as long as the servants puts their trust in their Lord.[25]

---

[24]If Allah do touch thee with hurt, there is none can remove it but He: if He do design some benefit for thee, there is none can keep back His favour: He causeth it to reach whomsoever of His servants He pleaseth. And He is the Oft-Forgiving, Most Merciful.
[25]If it had been thy Lord's will, they would all have believed - all who are on earth! wilt thou then compel mankind, against their will, to believe!

This beautiful surah reminds us that, while we may plan, it is not actually in our hands. This is not to say that we should not plan; on the contrary, we should make an effort to plan for years into our future, but we should remember that Allah's plan may be different from our own and that His plan is indeed better for us. As explained in verse 24, Allah (swt) may alter our plans to protect us from something bad or to steer us toward something good. [26]

In verses 35 and 36, He tells us not to seek guidance except from our Creator.[27] Oftentimes, we find ourselves frustrated because we do not have a manual for life. Allah has provided us with a manual—the Qur'an—if we choose to accept the wisdom and guidance it offers us, as well as the example of the Prophet. Allah concludes the surah by calling the believers to uphold peace as it is one of the first things Muslims should seek to establish. We must strive for peace within our own souls, within our mosques and communities and beyond.

In the last verse of Surah Yunus, Allah (swt) reminds us that seeking peace and spreading His word are incumbent upon the believers but in spite of the great efforts and sacrifices of our prophets, there will be those around us who continue to reject. We must never lose hope and should remain steadfast in

---

[26]The likeness of the life of the present is as the rain which We send down from the skies: by its mingling arises the produce of the earth-which provides food for men and animals: (It grows) till the earth is clad with its golden ornaments and is decked out (in beauty): the people to whom it belongs think they have all powers of disposal over it: There reaches it Our command by night or by day, and We make it like a harvest clean-mown, as if it had not flourished only the day before! thus do We explain the Signs in detail for those who reflect.
[27]Say: "Of your 'partners' is there any that can give any guidance towards truth?" Say: "It is Allah Who gives guidance towards truth, is then He Who gives guidance to truth more worthy to be followed, or he who finds not guidance (himself) unless he is guided? what then is the matter with you? How judge ye?" But most of them follow nothing but fancy: truly fancy can be of no avail against truth. Verily Allah is well aware of all that they do.

our efforts and *ibadah* and leave the remainder of Allah's plan to Him.

May Allah grant us patience in our struggles and may He make our final destination *Jannatul Firdous*.

Exercises for Surah Yunus

1. Everyone has a time of darkness or stress. This surah gives us hope in those times. In such times, make this the dua' you recite, "There is no god but You, Glory to You: I was indeed wrong!" (21:87)
2. As this surah teaches the importance of understanding how the language of the Qur'an was divinely protected, it reminds us that any time we hear about people threatening the Qur'an physically, it does not impact the Qur'an. It is still the protected word of Allah and remains in the heart of the Muslims.
3. In today's world we hear many people questioning the validity of certain verses in the Qur'an. Make a plan for how you can increase your understanding of the Qur'anic text. Learn a few words of Arabic or a few rules of grammar. Also, as you read through the Qur'an, write down verses that are difficult for you to understand. Set aside extra time to research and understand their context and meaning.
4. Remember that you cannot run from the decree of Allah. Allah's plan always prevails, so seek His assistance when it is needed; do not turn away from Him. Put your trust in Him in good times or "bad" and remind yourself in that moment that there is Allah's wisdom in all of His decrees.
5. Reflect on how much you take advantage of your time. Count how often Afterlife is on your mind when you plan how you will use your time throughout the day.

Surah Hud (11)

Surah Hud is a Makkan surah that was revealed in a time of great sorrow for our beloved Prophet (peace be upon him). Surah Hud followed the deaths of the Prophet's uncle Abu Talib and his wife Khadijah (may Allah be pleased with her).

This surah served as a comfort to him and a reminder to us of the difficulties faced by our prophets as well as the strength they gained after every challenge. It also gave clarity to the fact that the task of teaching this message is one of difficulty. It teaches us that life is a continuous test, one mountain after another; we must exercise endurance and patience, for those who never leave the foot of the mountain will never enjoy the splendor of its summit.

Surah Hud talks about the lives of many of the prophets: Hud, Salih, Shuayb, Lut, Musa, Ibrahim and Nuh. There is great focus on the story of Prophet Hud whom Allah sent to the people of 'Ad. The people of Ad were well known for their superiority over those around them and they believed there was no one more powerful than they. They carried themselves with arrogance and thought that it was their physical strength that caused them to be self-sufficient. They did not recognize that Allah (swt) was the one giving them power so He punished them by uprooting their entire civilization. Allah (swt) shows us in this story that it is not material power or physical power that serves as a criterion for greatness, but rather it is sincerity and *taqwa*, God consciousness, which raises our status in the eyes of Allah.

As we enjoy the benefits of Ramadan within a community of great blessing and influence, we must always remind ourselves that it is through remembrance of Allah and gratitude toward Him that we will gain His pleasure and reward. This story also served as a reminder to the Makkans that their power and wealth would not protect them from Allah (swt). The story warned them to turn to Allah in sincerity in order for Him to bless them and increase their possessions.

Prophet Hud (may Allah be pleased with Him) calls his people to seek forgiveness and to repent to Allah (swt) for their wrong doings. This reminds us that turning to Allah (swt) and seeking forgiveness does not make a person weak, rather it strengthens the person in every aspect. Surah Hud also reminds us that seeking forgiveness from Allah (swt) is not just a way to become closer to Him and purify our souls, but it is also an act of worship itself. The Prophet Muhammad (peace be upon him) was the most perfect of creations, yet he was known to have made *istighfar* 70 times a day, and some even say over a 100 times each day. This is a proof that seeking forgiveness draws us nearer to Allah. We should take the example and teachings of these two prophets and ask ourselves what we are we doing each day to distance ourselves from our mistakes and bring ourselves closer to our Creator.

Furthermore, in Surah Hud, verse 100, Allah tells us that He mentions these stories so that we may reflect upon them.[28] He reminds us that we will be held accountable on the Day of Judgment regarding how we managed what Allah blessed us with. Were we generous with our wealth? Did we abuse our power and strength? Did we give to those in need, aware that Allah is the one who provides and replenishes our provisions? Did we spread kindness and justice by way of our positions or status? Were we kind to our spouses, our parents, and our children?

Allah reminds us that the Day will come when we will wish that we had taken the time to reflect on these matters. But on that day, we will not be able to change our deeds. Ramadan is a time of self-evaluation and improvement. We must evaluate how we use each blessing granted to us and how it will speak

---

[28]These are some of the stories of communities which We relate unto thee: of them some are standing, and some have been mown down (by the sickle of time).

for us on the Day when all of humanity is gathered together to stand before Allah Almighty.

May Allah (swt) forgive our sins and bring us nearer to Him.

Exercises for Surah Hud

1. In some ways the Prophets struggled in the same way we do. In times of calamity or loss, turn back to this surah. Remember when reading it that these are the words that Allah sent down as comfort to our Beloved Prophet (peace be upon him). Let them be your words of comfort as well by reflecting on what parts of it brought comfort to him (peace be upon him).

2. The Prophet Muhammad (peace be upon him) made *istighfar* between 70 and 100 times per day. Try to make *istighfar* 20 times after each prayer. At the end of the five prayers you will have sought forgiveness to the equivalent amount of the most perfect man created. Once you have established this number, try to add more into your daily routine as each of us is far from perfect.

3. Identify people in your life who you are close to and who you can rely on to help you cope with difficulty by reminding you of Allah Almighty.

4. Reflect on these questions and what you are doing in your life in regards to them:
   a. Are you generous with your wealth and blessings, knowing that Allah is the one who provides and then replenishes your provisions?
   b. Do you abuse your power or strength?
   c. Did you spread kindness and speak up for justice?
   d. Are you kind to your spouse, parents, and children?

Surah Yusuf (12)

Like Surah Yunus and Surah Hud, this 12th surah of the Holy Qur'an was revealed in a strenuous and trying time in the life of the Prophet (peace be upon him). It was revealed just before the Hijrah, when Muslims were facing the most distressing times in Islamic history. It came as a reminder to the Prophet (peace be upon him) that difficulty comes to each person, but that difficulty is followed by ease and success. This surah was revealed around the same time as Surah Hud. They share the theme of mourning as Prophet Ya'qub was mourning the loss of his son Yusuf.

Surah Yusuf is one of the most beautiful stories in the Qur'an; Allah describes it as such in the third verse of the surah, as well as calling it the best of stories.[29] Unlike any others mentioned in the Qur'an, this story is unique in the sense that it was revealed and collected in its entirety in one surah. The story of Yusuf is a proof that Allah has created life as a test, one test after the other. Surah Yusuf is a story of a noble prophet who was the son of noble Yaqub, the son of noble Ishaq, the son of noble Ibrahim (may Allah be pleased with them all).

The story of Yusuf can be followed by the instances of the three shirts. The first shirt was of his childhood, which his brothers stained with false blood to show to their father. The second shirt came in his time as a young adult and is considered to be the shirt of innocence as it was proof of his innocence. The last shirt was the shirt of glad tidings and prosperity. It came at the time when Prophet Yusuf (may Allah be pleased with him) was reunited with his family, a symbol of his success and the beginning of ease for both Yusuf and his father (may Allah be pleased with them both).

---

[29]We do relate unto thee the most beautiful of stories, in that We reveal to thee this (portion of the) Qur'an: before this, thou too was among those who knew it not.

The story of Yusuf covers four important aspects of a Muslim's life. The first is dealing with difficulty within our own families. It discusses how the danger of jealousy can lead to grudges and hatred, stemming from lack of acceptance in the plan that Allah has decreed for us. The cure of jealousy is to dwell on what you have rather than dwelling on that which you do not have. We must look around ourselves at those who are not as fortunate as ourselves and be grateful for our blessings. A great scholar once said, "I have never been jealous of anyone. If it is a matter of *Dunya*, I know the *Dunya* doesn't last. If it is a matter of *Akhira*, how can I be jealous of something that I can attain through hard work?"

Another aspect this surah discusses is that of power and prosperity and, lastly, dealing with revenge and repentance. Prophet Yusuf (may Allah be pleased with him) faced all of these challenges throughout his life. He understood that Allah (swt) was testing him and he did not question Allah's plan. Each of us will go through struggles in our lives. We cannot compare one person's trials with another's but we must remember that Allah gradually increases the levels of our tests so that we may see the strength of our *Ihsan* (our relationship with Allah in terms of how it translates into action).

The story of Yusuf is an example of people conspiring to do wrong and reminding us that Allah is aware of their plot. Allah takes us on a journey through the struggles of Yusuf (peace be upon him) as he was betrayed by his own brothers, sold into slavery, and invited to sin. Yet his faith never wavered. Yusuf's moral character was tested as he was moved away from his family into a new and unfamiliar land as a slave. The faith that his father instilled in him carried him through his life of trials. This is a lesson to us that we must instill faith in the hearts of our children early in their lives. It does not suffice to send our children to Sunday school or Qur'an class once a week. We must exert the extra effort for them every day; to pray with them and talk to them about their Creator and to help them understand the actions of their beloved Prophet (may Allah be pleased with him) in order that they carry these lessons and wisdom with them into their adult lives. We must empower them to face challenges with Allah as their goal, confirming the lesson that Yaqub (may Allah be pleased with him) taught to his son: "Be conscious of Allah wherever you may be." We must remind them that, in public and private, Allah is ever watchful of all that we do, from the depth of the well, to the cells of prison, to the house of the king; Allah knows all things.

We also see from this beautiful relationship between father and child, that Yaqub (may Allah be pleased with him) was approachable. Yusuf was able to go to his father and address him without fear or anxiety about how his father would react. He was able to confide in him and seek his guidance. We must make ourselves available to our children—not only in terms of being physically present, which is important, but also emotionally available and open to anything they want to approach us about. Respond with consideration of their feelings and with the mindset to seek to understand their situation or concern.

When the wife of the 'Aziz approached Prophet Yusuf, he saw the spiritual aspect that she was blind to. Prophet Yusuf understood that the attainment of Allah's pleasure was greater than that of any worldly pleasure. He asked Allah to protect him from engaging in sin. As a result, Yusuf was unjustly imprisoned, yet he remained truthful to his faith even in the most difficult of circumstances.

But it was not in prison that Yusuf faced his greatest test, nor was it in the depths of the well; the real test came to him when he was asked to assist the king in interpreting a dream. It was at that time that Yusuf (may Allah be pleased with him) gained the upper hand through his ability to interpret dreams. Yusuf was faced with three choices: the first was refusing to interpret the dream until he was released from prison; misinterpreting the dream in order to get revenge; or lastly, overlooking the wrong against him and seeking the greater good. Prophet Yusuf chose to overlook the injustice against him, expressing his strong love for humanity. This exemplifies his ability to overcome his own pain and extend his hand to his enemy, as love is more powerful than revenge and forgiveness is greater than getting even. Yusuf (may Allah be pleased with him) showed an exceptional ability to control anger and forgive his own brothers when they came to him seeking help. He did not take advantage of the situation. He forgave them and asked Allah to forgive them.

The story of Yusuf (may Allah be pleased with him) is exceptional in the number of lessons in character it provides. But another aspect to this story is that of the relationship between Prophet Yusuf and his father, Yaqub (may Allah be pleased with them both). The love between the father and his child is so intense that, after Yusuf was taken from his family, his father grieved for him to the point that his eyes are described as having turned white. This also shows that it is permissible for Muslims to grieve, to feel pain when a loved one is taken from them, but Yaqub also teaches us, through his example, that we must never question Allah (swt) when He chooses something for us. We know that the Prophet Muhammad (peace be upon him) showed sadness at the loss of his wife Khadijah, his son Ibrahim, his uncle Abu Talib, and his cousin Hamza—who were all pillars of strength for him—but returned to Allah during his life. Yaqub (may Allah be pleased with him) also modeled a positive relationship with his other children though they had caused the pain that he felt. He maintained a good relationship with them, still trying with all of his effort to guide them back to Allah. Yusuf (may Allah be pleased with him) later became a minister of the land, a just and fair minister of the country's wealth. We must remember to worship Allah (swt) in times of both difficulty and prosperity.

Exercises for Surah Yusuf

---

1. Engage your children:
   a. Set aside time for your children to have an open discussion with you. Let them express what they would like to, their fears, concerns, and their dreams. Be both physically and emotionally available to your children as Prophet Yaqub was for his son Yusuf (peace be upon them).
   b. Read the stories of the prophets with your children from a young age. Help them connect the stories to their everyday lives and situations; teach them patience through the story of Nuh, conviction through the story of Yusuf, and compassion through the story of Muhammad (peace be upon them all).
   c. Show your children they are loved despite the errors they may make.
2. Jealousy and sibling rivalry:
   Take your children to see the situation of those less fortunate than they are. This will help them appreciate the things they have rather than focus on what they do not.
3. Dealing with injustice:
   a. Remember that you may not always see justice being served. Justice is with Allah. Prophet Yusuf was in jail approximately 10 years. Write down injustices that have been done to you that you still hold onto. Be objective about what took place. Then let them go.
   b. Remember that anger prevents you from moving forward and is a motivator for revenge. Continuously remember Allah and seek protection from the whispers of Shaytan when you feel angry in order to overcome and move past being wronged.

      c.   Never use the upper hand for revenge.
      d.   Interact with the people who wronged you so you allow yourself the chance to forgive them.
      e.   Ask Allah to forgive those who wronged you. Making *dua'* for them will make it easier to forgive them.
      f.   Help those who are suffering from injustice in your community and around the world.

4. Beware of your environment:
   How do you deal with the environment that is tempting or testing your faith? Reflect on whether the Qur'an is the criterion for you in all situations or does your criterion for right and wrong change based on whom you are with.
5. Understand that Allah can give tests one at a time or in succession. The way for passing tests is through gratitude and patience.
6. Evaluate if greed is ever the motivator in doing right or wrong.

Surah Ar Ra'ad (13)

Surah Ar Ra'ad is a Madinan surah. It follows Surah Yusuf in discussing the characteristics of the Qur'an and attributes of Allah (swt). Surah Ar Ra'ad is a very powerful surah covering five important themes: connecting to truth, being conscious of Allah, changing of our conditions, and naming of the surahs of the Qur'an and *Dhikr*. This is the first surah in the order of compilation that is named after a phenomenon. Ra'ad means thunder. The rain following thunder can be Allah's merciful rain that brings fruits or it can bring destructive floods.

Allah (swt) confirms in Surah Ar Ra'ad that the Message of the Prophet Muhammad (peace be upon him) and the Prophet himself are true. He confirms that the Book of Revelation and the Signs of Allah are true. Allah (swt) connects us with the signs that are visible to us in this world: the sun, the moon, the thunder, the mountain, the rivers, the fruits and so much more, in order that we may try to understand. Allah has made these signs for us to reflect upon and to remember Him.

Each morning when we wake up the sun provides the world around us with light to see and at night Allah shows His greatness by removing the light and putting us in darkness. Yet He provides the light of the stars and the moon to guide us. For those who take the time to reflect upon these signs, they will see that Allah has placed the stars, not only as a guide for our eyes to see this world at night, but as a guide for our hearts to see the Truth of His power and His mercy. Allah (swt) also reminds us in this surah that there are those amongst us who see these signs and reject them. Their attribution of these signs to others besides Allah by no means negates the truth.

In verse eight, He gives the example of the womb of the mother, a place of such extraordinary secrecy.[30] The mother herself does not know the state of the child and the child, after being brought into the world, will remember nothing of his being in the womb of his mother. Yet Allah is well aware of every detail of such things. He (swt) cares for the child and the mother in this vulnerable time in their lives. In these signs and miracles, Allah removes all reason for doubt of His existence. He proclaims in the following verse that, whether we choose to believe or not believe, Allah is the Knower of all that is in the physical world and all that is in the world of the Unseen.

We have been reminded many times in the surahs leading to this surah that this life is full of trials. Many people who question the existence of Allah come back to the same question: "Why does evil exist?" In verse 11, Allah (swt) explains

---

[30]Allah doth know what every female (womb) doth bear, by how much the wombs fall short (of their time or number) or do exceed. Every single thing is before His sight, in (due) proportion.

the social law that has been established.[31] Allah does not change the condition of a people until they change the condition of themselves, within their own souls. This is in reference to both the individual and the group, but also refers to matters which we have the power to change. People engage in habits and behavior that Allah has warned as being destructive. Then when our bodies, our emotions, or our faith are brought down, we question Allah as to why it happened. Allah did not ask us to engage in those activities; on the contrary, He warned us to avoid them as much as possible. A person might also raise the question as to why "bad things happen to good people." The meaning behind this is that good and sincere individuals face times of difficulty and loss. Allah (swt) has reminded us many times, especially in the story of our beloved Prophet Yusuf (peace be upon him), that even good people will face trial. There are matters that Allah has decreed that are entirely out of our control, but we are not in such situations as a result of any wrongdoing, but merely as a test of our commitment to Allah. If we look at this in the light of the earlier verses of this surah, trials and tribulations are opportunities for gaining nearness to Allah Almighty, if we choose to respond to them in appropriate ways.

Throughout the surahs of the Qur'an, Allah (swt) reminds us that we will have times of prosperity and times of difficulty; each in their own ways is a test of our faith. Allah has also reminded us that the Qur'an is a source of remedies for whatever we may face. After having warned us of the trials, He provides us with a key to navigating through them. In verse 28 of Surah Ar Ra'ad, Allah (swt) reminds the believers: "Those who believe, and whose hearts find satisfaction in the remembrance

---

[31]For each (such person) there are (angels) in succession, before and behind him: They guard him by command of Allah. Verily never will Allah change the condition of a people until they change it themselves (with their own souls). But when (once) Allah willeth a people's punishment, there can be no turning it back, nor will they find, besides Him, any to protect.

of Allah: for without doubt in the remembrance of Allah do hearts find satisfaction." Allah is reminding us that whatever comes our way in life, it is through remembrance of Him that we will find happiness and satisfaction. If we are in times of difficulty and our minds and hearts turn to the remembrance of Allah, we will be able to put into perspective our difficulties. We will remember that this life is just temporary and all that is in it will come to an end. If we remember Him in times of prosperity, we will enjoy the blessings He has provided and we will not dwell on the human desire for more.

O Allah, let us see truth as truth and follow it and let us see falsehood as falsehood and help us turn away from it.

Exercises for Surah Ar Ra'ad

1. Sit outside on a night that the moon is not visible. Remember how dark the night is. Go outside again, on a night when the moon is full and the stars are visible. Reflect on the physical and spiritual meaning of the moon and the stars as a guide in times of darkness.

2. Reflect on times that you habitually fall into error or transgress. Evaluate the steps that get you there and take responsibility to cut off those steps in the future.

3. If you find yourself relying on someone other than Allah, go to a fountain or faucet and try collecting water to drink in an open hand. It will result in you feeling unfulfilled.

4. Have a routine of *dhikr*, other than the sunnah, that you do every morning, every night, or when you have nothing else to do. By practicing the remembrance of Allah in good times, in times of difficulty His remembrance will roll off your tongue and comfort your heart.

5. When you feel depleted spiritually, remind yourself that "Verily in the remembrance of Allah, do hearts find

ease". Remove the thought of a test being a punishment and look at it as what it is, an opportunity to strengthen your relationship with Allah.

6. Say this *dua'* the next time you hear thunder: "How perfect He is (the One) for Whom the thunder declares His perfection with His praise, as do the angels out of fear of Him."

7. Say this *dua'* the next time it rains: "O Allah, send upon us helpful wholesome and healthy rain, beneficial not harmful rain."

Surah Ibrahim (14)

Surah Ibrahim is named after one of the greatest Prophets of Allah. Prophet Ibrahim (peace be upon him) was one of the founders of Makkah and the people of Makkah were easily able to identify with him, as he was from amongst their own. This Makkan surah discusses *Aqidah*, or "creed," the Day of Resurrection, and discusses the purpose of the Prophethood.

The earlier verses explain the purpose of the Qur'an, to deliver humanity from darkness to light, and explain how Allah (swt) has sent the prophets as guides to humanity. Their purpose was to convey the Message but, as we see through their stories, they were not made to force people to believe in Allah and the Last Day. The prophets were sent to live the message of Allah. The message was unique but the prophets, like those they preached to, were no more than human creations of Allah. Allah sent His prophets to serve as guides to His path, but there were still those who rejected. They did not want to see the signs.

As we sit here engaging in the benefits of Ramadan, we are of those whom Allah (swt) has shown the path. It is now up to us to advance our position on that path by engaging in *ibadah*, worship, and *dhikr*, remembrance of Allah (swt), even after the month of Ramadan has passed. Allah has explained to the believers many times that the line of communication with Allah is always open. Why do some amongst us only choose to speak with Him in this month? Allah (swt)—our Creator, our Provider, our source of ease and comfort—is the same Merciful God throughout the year as He is in Ramadan; should we not then be the same loyal servants? Allah reminds us in verse 34 that those who seek from Him with sincerity and true faith will be given all that they ask for.[32] What we must remind ourselves is that we cannot always see the response from Allah, as there are times when the answer to our *du'a* is being saved for the next life. But this is part of the belief that the servant must have in his Lord; Allah knows best what we need to be given and He knows what our spiritual soul needs for Him to withhold. We must take the same advice that Allah (swt) gave to His messengers in verse 47 of Surah Ibrahim: "Never think that Allah would fail His messengers in His promise; For Allah is Exalted in Power—The Lord of Retribution." There is no situation or test in this world that will pass without Allah's knowledge. He has promised to hear and respond to the prayer of anyone who seeks His assistance.

For many of us, our *Ibadah*, worship, is more intense in this blessed month. For others, it is the only time that we engage in *Ibadah*. Whose pleasure are we seeking for the rest of the year? Allah reminds us in verses 21 and 22 of Surah Ibrahim that there will be those on earth who lead people astray.[33] We

---

[32]And He giveth you of all that ye ask for. But if ye count the favours of Allah, never will ye be able to number them. Verily, man is given up to injustice and ingratitude.

[33]They will all be marshalled before Allah together: then will the weak say to those who were arrogant, "For us, we but followed you; can ye then avail us to all against the wrath of Allah." They will reply, "If we had received the Guidance of Allah, we should have given it to you: to us it makes no difference (now) whether we rage, or bear (these torments) with patience: for ourselves there is no way of escape."
And Satan will say when the matter is decided: "It was Allah Who gave you a promise of Truth: I too promised, but I failed in my promise to you. I had no authority over you except to call you but ye listened to me: then reproach not me, but reproach your own souls. I cannot listen to your cries, nor can ye listen to mine. I reject your former act

must protect ourselves from being followers of those people. For Allah reminds us that on the Day of Judgment such leaders will be accountable for what they did. While they may have welcomed our company in this life, on that Day they will forget their followers and will not be any source of protection. Shaytan has promised to try and remove us from the path of Allah. However, even he admits that we were the ones who wronged ourselves. He says, "I had no authority over you except to call you, but you listened to me." Again in this surah, Allah is warning us of a danger and, out of His love for His servant, He is providing us with a solution. In verse 31, Allah tells us to establish regular prayer and spend out of what He has provided to us.[34] Allah further emphasizes the importance of the establishment of prayer by conveying to the believers that the best *Da'wah* is that of one who establishes prayer with his children. Prophet Ibrahim is an example of the best way to do this. We cannot simply ask our children to pray. We have to model the actions we want to see in them. It is through such devotion to Allah and sacrifice of that which is dear to us, that we will find ourselves able to stand before Him on the day when He is our only source of hope.

May Allah guide us on His path and protect us from deviation. May He grant us all that is good for us and protect us from that which removes us from His light.

Exercises for Surah Ibrahim

1. Pick a "buddy" from your family or friends and make a pledge with that friend for something you will engage in

---

in associating me with Allah. For wrong-doers there must be a grievous penalty."

[34]Speak to my servants who have believed, that they may establish regular prayers, and spend (in charity) out of the sustenance we have given them, secretly and openly, before the coming of a Day in which there will be neither mutual bargaining nor befriending.

outside of Ramadan to increase your connection to Allah.

2. The Qur'an is intended to be applied into life. Make it a habit when reading the Qur'an to read the translation and the *tafsir* so you can understand the full meaning and how to apply it.

3. Make *dua'* for absolutely anything you want or need, and know in your heart that Allah responds to every supplication. Continue to make *dua'* that the injustice we see in the world today will be eliminated and do not allow yourself to ever believe that Allah is not aware of injustice. He is aware and hears our calls but Allah (swt) has his own time to hold wrongdoers accountable.

4. When you find yourself attributing a wrong action to Shaytan's whispers remind yourself of what Shaytan himself said: "I had no authority over you except to call you, but you listened to me: then reproach not me, but reproach your own souls."

5. Make it a habit to pray with your children and if they are too young to pray, pray in an area that they can see you. Do not just tell your children to pray, help them to learn from your example.

Surah Al Hijr (15)

Surah Al Hijr is the last of the six surahs beginning with the letters *"Alif Lam Meem"* or *"Alif Lam Ra"*. It is a Makkan surah that was revealed shortly after the revelation of Surah Yusuf, a time of great trials for the Muslim community just before the Hijrah to Madinah. The title "Al Hijr" is taken from the 80th verse of the surah.[35] It can refer to a geographic location, the northernmost area of the Hijaz between Madinah and Syria, or the tribe of Thamud, to whom Prophet Salih was sent. Surah Al Hijr uses the stories of Prophets Ibrahim and Lut (peace be upon them both) to examine the regret of the disbelievers on the Day

---

[35]The Companions of the Rocky Tract also rejected the apostles:

73

of Judgment, the protection of Allah's message and the protection of the truth, the evil of Shaytan and the difficulties the unbelievers had placed upon the prophets of Allah to try to weaken them.

Allah (swt) opens this surah with three letters, the meaning of which we cannot be certain about. He immediately moves to discussing the regret the disbelievers will face on the Day of Judgment. They will wish they had believed but their regret will come too late. As Allah (swt) explains in the third verse, they will wish they had embraced Islam and bowed down in worship. Sadly, even today, we see many Muslims compromising the commands of Allah in order to enjoy aspects of the *Dunya* that are beyond the boundaries of Islam. After time, they attempt to use unauthentic interpretations of the words of Allah to justify their transgressions. Allah is indicating here that, whatever we do, we will inevitably be asked to justify our actions before Him, and He knows well what is in His book and what is in our hearts.

The disbelievers from the times of the prophets did what they could to convince themselves that the Message was false. As was discussed in an earlier surah, the language of the Qur'an was so unique that the Arabs were not able to counter the message by attacking the Qur'an itself. In a way this was an acknowledgement on their part of the uniqueness of the Qur'an. As a result, the disbelievers turned from attacking the message to attacking the messengers. In verses 8 and 9, they accuse Prophet Muhammad (peace be upon him) of being a madman and ask him to bring down the angels to prove he is conveying the truth.[36] But Allah reveals that the angels are not sent down to satisfy their curiosity or entertain their arrogant

---

[36]We send not the angels down except for just cause: if they came (to the ungodly), behold! no respite would they have! We have, without doubt, sent down the Message; and We will assuredly guard it (from corruption).

suggestions. Rather, angels were on a mission to provide inspiration to the Messengers of Allah. He (swt) responds to their audacious remarks with a powerful statement in verse 22 of Surah Al Furqan: "On the Day that they do see the angels, there will be no good news given on that day to the guilty. And the angels will say: 'All kinds of glad tidings are forbidden for you.'" The disbelievers questioned the messengers as to why Allah had not sent them in the form of a more powerful being if they were indeed the Messengers of Allah. What they did not realize was what a great blessing it was to have the model of good and righteousness walking the earth in the form of a human. It allows us to believe that we are able to attain what the prophets would preach. Would we follow the Prophet Muhammad (peace be upon him) in fasting if he was a being that did not require sustenance? Would we relate to his emotions if he went through life and did not feel sadness? Allah, in His infinite Wisdom, understands the human need to relate and feel connected, so He granted us prophets like ourselves. As we travel through the stories of the Qur'an we must remember that while the prophets were superior human beings, they were still human beings. We must use the examples they left behind to establish and increase our *Iman*.

Surah Al Hijr explains the Seven Gates of Hell. The followers of Shaytan have each been assigned a gate according to the weight of their deeds. The intensity of the descriptions of Hell should shake the heart of any reader. The punishment is severe and Allah reminds us of Shaytan's vow to cause people to stray. But in verse 42, Allah says to Shaytan, "For over My servants no authority shall you have, except such as put themselves in the wrong and follow you." It is made clear here that our wrongdoings cannot be blamed on anyone other than ourselves. Shaytan may invite us to sin but the decision to engage is our own.

Verses 45-49 then speak about the People of Paradise

and the reward they are granted for their efforts in this world.[37] These verses describe the beautiful images of Paradise and remind us that Allah will make it perfect for each person. Any displeasure with their life in this world will be resolved and Allah will grant His servant all that he wanted in this life and more. No harm will come to the people of Paradise.

This surah puts into perspective our life on earth. Allah has granted us the Prophets as examples of what we should be. He warns us of Shaytan's promise and that the decision to follow him or follow Allah remains in our hands, and He makes clear the two options we have for the *Akhirah*. We must reflect on what are we doing and where our actions are taking us. May Allah forgive our sins and protect us from the punishment of the Fire.

Exercises for Surah Hijr

1. Do not let the material world distract you from the beauty of the message and do not exchange the blessings it promises for worldly things.
   a. If you find yourself leaning towards something that distances you from the pleasure of Allah, say to yourself, "I chose Allah above such and such thing." You will avoid regret in that moment and on the Day of Judgment.

---

[37] Hast thou not turned thy vision to thy Lord?- How He doth prolong the shadow! If He willed, He could make it stationary! then do We make the sun its guide; Then We draw it in towards Ourselves,- a contraction by easy stages
And He it is Who makes the Night as a Robe for you, and Sleep as Repose, and makes the Day (as it were) a Resurrection.
And He it is Who sends the winds as heralds of glad tidings, going before His mercy, and We send down pure water from the sky,- That with it We may give life to a dead land, and slake the thirst of things We have created,- cattle and men in great numbers.

    b.   If you feel that the whispers of Shaytan are getting to you, say "I seek refuge in Allah from Shaytan the accursed."

Surah An Nahl (16)

Surah An Nahl is a Makkan surah that discusses the immense amount of blessings that Allah (swt) has bestowed upon His servants. In fact, the blessings of Allah are mentioned so many times that the surah is also known as Surah Ni'aam, or the Surah of Bounties.

The title of the surah comes from verses 68 and 69 where Allah talks about the blessing of the bees.[38] Allah taught the bees how to function as a collective unit to build a hive and produce honey in it. Allah reminds us that from these small creatures He brings a substance of healing for humankind. Allah has made one of the smallest creatures so beneficial to the greatest creature on Earth. He (swt) also speaks in this surah about His Lordship, the revelation, and the resurrection.

Allah (swt) talks about the many different blessings He has bestowed upon us, from the rain to the vegetation, and the animals that we ride to the animals we consume. He has mentioned all of these things and all of the purposes for which we need them in order to earn a livelihood and sustain ourselves. He talks about the birds, the shade, the hills, our homes and our clothes. He talks about the balance that He has placed in the universe in order for us to function within the vast system that is working around us.

All too often we do not show gratitude. Indeed, the

---

[38] And thy Lord taught the Bee to build its cells in hills, on trees, and in (men's) habitations; Then to eat of all the produce (of the earth), and find with skill the spacious paths of its Lord: there issues from within their bodies a drink of varying colours, wherein is healing for men: verily in this is a Sign for those who give thought.

most severe form of ingratitude to Allah (swt) is to be anything other than just to His creations. In verse 59, Allah (swt) makes mention of the *Jahiliya* tradition of female infanticide.[39] The Arabs would give themselves two choices following the birth of a daughter: the first was to keep her alive, and as they allowed themselves to see it, in shame and disgrace; and the second was to bury her alive. What could be a more hideous form of ingratitude? Unfortunately, similar things still happen in the world today. Some people do choose to abort a pregnancy if they find the child to be a girl; others keep their daughters, but treat them more like property than people.

The Qur'an also emphasizes the women's right of education and free will, marriage by choice, and equal status in society. In verse 97, Allah shows that in regards to deeds, men and women are equal in the eyes of Allah.[40] We as humans cannot lessen, merely for our convenience and desire to control, the status of something that Allah has determined to be equal.

Furthermore, Muslims are commanded to act justly with all creatures, not only human beings. Allah (swt) tells us to benefit from the nature around us. To be appreciative of this is to protect it from abuse and destruction. Unfortunately, we see too many cases of abuse against animals. Allah sees our ingratitude and removes the blessings from our care as we are only mishandling them. We see this through diseases such as Mad Cow disease and Bird Flu, and other illnesses that spread amongst animals and people.

In verse 83, Allah (swt) reminds us of the unfortunate truth, that many of us see the blessings of Allah in front of us

---

[39]With shame does he hide himself from his people, because of the bad news he has had! Shall he retain it on (sufferance and) contempt, or bury it in the dust? Ah! what an evil (choice) they decide on?
[40]Whoever works righteousness, man or woman, and has Faith, verily, to him will We give a new Life, a life that is good and pure and We will bestow on such their reward according to the best of their actions.

every day, yet we walk pass them without a degree of gratitude.[41] It is impossible for us as humans to show appreciation to Allah for everything that He has given us but it is necessary for us to contemplate and recognize where we would be without so many of His gifts. How often do we think about the absence of pain in our bodies, the strength of our muscles? How often do we think about the saliva that allows us to swallow, or the tears that keep our eyes from drying? How often do we thank Allah for our parents and our children and our families? For many, if we start now and thank Allah for these things each time we find ourselves complaining about them, we will have multiplied our gratitude many times.

In verse 121, Allah tells us of the reward of Prophet Ibrahim (peace be upon him), a model of an appreciative servant. Allah says for them is the good in this world and the next and the grateful servants are in the ranks of the righteous.[42]

Verses 53 and 54 mention the servants who are grateful when it is convenient for them.[43] When we are touched with calamity, we call on Allah and ask for His Bounties, as we know He is the only source. Allah responds to our call and grants His bounties, but we are not mindful and we quickly turn back to what we were doing, neglecting to thank Him.

"And if you were to count up the favors of Allah, never would you be able to count them, for Allah is Oft Forgiving, Most Merciful." [16:18]

---

[41]They recognise the favours of Allah. then they deny them; and most of them are (creatures) ungrateful.
[42]He showed his gratitude for the favours of Allah, who chose him, and guided him to a Straight Way.
[43]And ye have no good thing but is from Allah. and moreover, when ye are touched by distress, unto Him ye cry with groans; Yet, when He removes the distress from you, behold! some of you turn to other gods to join with their Lord-

1. Remember that men and women are equal in earning good deeds.
2. Have everyone in your family keep a journal throughout the year. Each evening before you sleep, write down one or two things for which you feel particularly grateful on that day. Come back to this journal in times that you feel you are being tested or that Allah is withholding something from you. Remind yourself of all the blessings He has given you.
3. Help your family be aware of the source of the blessings in your home, from food and drink to furniture and cars. Recognize the *rizq* of Allah.

Surah Isra' (17)

Surah Isra' is a Makkan surah. It speaks about the most beautiful and spiritual journey of the Prophet Muhammad (peace be upon him). This surah was revealed after the difficult events of Ta'if, in which the Prophet was pelted with stones to the point that his feet were covered with blood.

Surah Isra' covers the event of Isra' and Mi'raj, when the beloved Prophet of Allah was taken from Masjid Al Haraam in Makkah to Masjid Al Aqsa in Jerusalem, and then ascended to Heaven, returning over the duration of one night, making a connection between these two sacred mosques. The Mi'raj was thought to be on the 27th night of Rajab in the year before the Hijrah.

This surah talks about the spiritual experiences, or tests, that the prophets went through. It reminds us of the unity of the one true religion and that all the prophets came with the same message. The Prophet has explained to us the significance of these two sacred mosques when he (peace be upon him) said, "No one should make pilgrimage or special effort to visit the holy site, except Masjid al Haraam, Masjid an-Nabi and Masjid Al Aqsa."

Allah (swt) is taking the reader on a spiritual journey. He begins the surah by reminding us in verse 9 that He has provided the Qur'an as a guide for the believers to do what is right and good.[44] Ramadan is a time during which our interaction with the Qur'an increases. Allah has sent it as a guide; will we not seek the guidance from it after Ramadan? Is the Qur'an only something we use for special occasions? Our challenge is to contemplate our relationship with the Qur'an throughout the rest of the year. Is interacting with the Qur'an a part of our everyday life as it should be?

It is not sufficient just to be in a house where the *Mushaf* is present. The Qur'an is not something for us to read or listen to from time to time; it is something for us to interact with. We are in need of the guidance as Allah reminds us in verses 13 and 14 that, ultimately, the responsibility of every single one of our actions is on us alone.[45] We cannot depend on the religiosity of our family members or friends to earn our reward or save us from punishment as Allah says, "Every man's fate We have fastened on his own neck." Imagine a book in which every single one of our smallest deeds is documented; each uttered word, each deed, each thought.

Verses 22 to 38 outline the 10 beautiful commandments of Islam, including *Tawhid*, kindness to parents, prohibition

---

[44]Verily this Qur'an doth guide to that which is most right (or stable), and giveth the Glad Tidings to the Believers who work deeds of righteousness, that they shall have a magnificent reward;

[45]Every man's fate We have fastened on his own neck: On the Day of Judgment We shall bring out for him a scroll, which he will see spread open. (It will be said to him:) "Read thine (own) record: Sufficient is thy soul this day to make out an account against thee."

against taking human life, and being mindful of our wealth by not over-spending and not being stingy.

Exercises for Surah Isra

1. Try to experience the spiritual ascension in our prayers that the Prophet Muhammad (peace be upon him) experienced in Isra' and Mi'raj.
2. Practice increased kindness towards your parents.
   a. Speak in a softened and respectful tone.
   b. Do not say "*uff*", or use other expressions of your displeasure
   c. Refrain from talking back to them.
   d. Also refrain from showing any sort of non verbal disrespect.
   e. Each time you speak to them address them with their title as mother or father (by whichever name you normally address them). This will remind you of their honored status in relation to who you are.
   f. Keep a picture of you and your parents from your childhood somewhere where you are often reminded of it. Think of what they did for you and how it is now time for you to reciprocate that kindness and caring to them.
3. Commit to making the Qur'an a regular part of your routine. If you only read it in Ramadan, start to read it once a month. If you already read once a month, try once a week. If you already do that, try once a day. Be patient with yourself in establishing a new routine so that you do not become overwhelmed by it.

5

Surah Al Kahf to Surah An Naml

Surah Al Kahf (18)

Surah Al Kahf is a Makkan surah revealed in the last year before Hijrah. Surah Al Kahf consists of many stories that serve as parables to mankind. They remind us of goodness and virtue built around belief in Allah. It is a reminder of the importance of detaching our hearts from this life, as it is only a brief moment. These allegories teach us the importance of guarding the spiritual soul and preventing any passage of evil into our hearts.

The first of the stories involves the source of the surah's name, that of the people of the Cave. These young men sought refuge in this cave from their people for the sake of their religion. The word *"Raqim"* is understood by some scholars to refer to the mountain of the cave, while others interpret it to refer to the tablet with their stories. These youth entered the cave and supplicated to Allah to bestow on them His Mercy and Kindness. They had placed their faith in Allah and left Him to take care of them. As a result, Allah caused them to sleep. Allah (swt) explains in verse 11 that He sealed their ears to prevent them from hearing the commotion of the world around them, and placed the darkness of the cave as a cover for their eyes.[46] The seven youth remained unconscious of any passing of time for generations—309 years. When the cave was being demolished, they were awakened, unaware of the changes that took place in the world around them, or the amount of time that had passed while they slept.

---

[46]Then We draw (a veil) over their ears, for a number of years, in the Cave, (so that they heard not):

Each of the youth had interpreted the amount of time that had passed differently from the other, but they did not quarrel over their differences. This is a lesson to us that we need not dispute over such matters, as our internal experiences will cause us to see things from more than one perspective. It is better to say, "Allah knows best," and leave it at that. Allah tells us the story is of these young men to emphasize the importance of their sacrifice for Him. They did not have the same stature as others around them because they were so young. The elders amongst them were set on worshipping idols and had no desire to change. The youth took into their hands the authority to make the decision to leave falsehood and evil, to follow the path of Allah. This story should be an example to our own youth that Allah demands respect and kindness to our elders, particularly our parents. However, in matters that are in contradiction to Allah's commands, He has given the youth the power and intelligence to make the correct decision. Another lesson to be taken from this story is that belief in Allah and dedication to worship and trust in Him will lead to what is right and will protect us against companions of Shaytan.

Another major story of Surah Al Kahf is that of the teacher of Musa (peace be upon him). This surah deals with the importance of understanding people around you and having humility and respect for all types of knowledge.

Musa (peace be upon him) is guided to his teacher, Al Khidr. Upon meeting his teacher, Musa (peace be upon him) asks in a gentle and kind manner, "May I follow you?"—meaning he wanted to follow Al Khidr and spend time with him. This is a lesson for us to seek knowledge when the opportunity comes before us. It also tells us of the manner in which the student addresses the teacher, with ease and kindness, rather than in any forceful manner. Al Khidr responds by acknowledging the difference of the knowledge that each possesses; he understands that Musa (peace be upon him) has knowledge of the texts but has no knowledge of the new land he will visit. In this story we see again, disagreement without disrespect and harshness. Al Khidr tells Musa (peace be upon him) not to argue with him on matters he disagrees with, as Khidr knows better the people they will interact with than Musa does. Musa does not pass judgment on the people and proceeds. We should also make sure to refrain from making judgments. When we visit others' homes or communities, we must not pass judgment, as we are not knowledgeable of their situations. We must first try to understand the context in which their choices are made.

In verse 77, Allah (swt) explains the situation in which Al Khidr and Musa (peace be upon him) come upon the people of the town.[47] The people contradict the established customs of hospitality by not offering their guests anything. Furthermore, when Musa and his teacher request a share of their food, they refuse. Sadly, many of us would then launch verbal attacks on those who acted in a rude manner, or in some other way express dislike for their lack of generosity. Al Khidr teaches us a lesson of which every Muslim and non-Muslim should be mindful. Al Khidr responds to people of the town by walking away from them to a torn down wall within the town's borders. The broken wall had been built to protect the vulnerable inhabitants of the land. He repairs the wall and leaves the people. Al Khidr completed an act of charity despite how he was treated. How many of us react in such a manner? This is the teacher of a Prophet—should we not take lessons from his example? We must remember that, though others may be unjust towards us, reacting with the same action is not any better. Two wrongs never make a right.

---

[47]Then they proceeded: until, when they came to the inhabitants of a town, they asked them for food, but they refused them hospitality. They found there a wall on the point of falling down, but he set it up straight. (Moses) said: "If thou hadst wished, surely thou couldst have exacted some recompense for it!"

Exercises for Surah Al Kahf

---

1. Read verses 45-59 and imagine the events of the *Qiyama* as described in those verses.
2. Encourage the youth in your life to reflect on this story and see how Allah (swt) cares for the youth who struggle to stay on His path.

Surah Maryam (19)

Surah Maryam is a Makkan surah that was revealed nine years before the Hijrah, in the fifth year of Prophethood. Surah Maryam takes its name from verse 16: "Relate in the Book (the story of) Mary. When she withdrew from her family to a place in the East."

Surah Maryam talks about the people of the Book, the Muslim belief in 'Isa, Jesus, (peace be upon him), and the relationship between Ibrahim (peace be upon him) and his father when calling his father to Islam. Surah Maryam, of course, also addresses Maryam, the mother of 'Isa (peace be upon her). This is the only surah in the Qur'an that is named after a woman. It shows how honored the mother of Jesus is in Islam.

Ja'fir ibn Abi Talib, the cousin of the Prophet (peace be upon him), was sent to the King of Abyssinia when the persecution of the Muslims had reached its peak. They were seeking protection from the Christian king in the first contact that the Muslim Ummah had with the Christian community. Ja'fir Ibn Abi Talib recited Surah Maryam to the King, at which point the King drew a line on the ground. He said to Ja'fir Ibn Abi Talib, "This is the difference between us," and then refused to turn the Muslims away. This shows how just a king he was, and the comfort that he was able to provide to the Muslims in a time of such great difficulty. We, as Muslims today, should remember the kindness of the Christian king to the Muslims and should exercise the same kindness amongst ourselves, as well as across the lines of religion. We may have our differences, but kindness crosses the boundaries of every kind. It is not a matter of religion; it is a matter of humanity.

Similarly, in verses 45-47, Allah shows the dialogue between Ibrahim (may Allah be pleased with him) and his father as he tried to bring him to Islam and away from idol worshipping.[48] Ibrahim invited his father with kindness; he did not curse him or force him. The father of the prophet responded to him with threats. Prophet Ibrahim answered him by saying "Peace be onto you." This is an example of the type of dialogue that Muslims should engage in between family members and in interfaith interactions. Prophet Ibrahim maintained his patience even when being threatened. He listened to what was said and responded in the manner that he knew would be pleasing to Allah, not in a manner of anger or retaliation.

This surah also talks about the struggles of Maryam (may Allah be pleased with her). She had to leave her family and seclude herself from people to pray and devote herself to Allah. It was during this time that she was visited by the angel who informed her she would give birth to a blessed son. Maryam gave birth to Prophet 'Isa, and we are reminded throughout the Qur'an of her status as his mother and that 'Isa (may Allah be pleased with him) did not have any father. Allah refers to Prophet 'Isa throughout the Qur'an as "'Isa, the son of Maryam," even when the tradition was to refer to a child by the name of the father, not the mother. In this, Allah is also establishing an honorable rank for the mother of 'Isa (peace be upon them both). As Allah (swt) explained in Surah Al Imran, she is the most

---

[48]"O my father! I fear lest a Penalty afflict thee from ((Allah)) Most Gracious, so that thou become to Satan a friend." (The father) replied: "Dost thou hate my gods, O Abraham? If thou forbear not, I will indeed stone thee: Now get away from me for a good long while!" Abraham said: "Peace be on thee: I will pray to my Lord for thy forgiveness: for He is to me Most Gracious.

honored of women.

Surah Maryam describes the birth of the beloved Prophet 'Isa (may Allah be pleased with him). His birth was a miraculous sign that billions of people believe in. While there are differences in interpretation, this moment of birth shows the human aspect of Maryam and 'Isa. Maryam (peace be upon her) brought her son to her people and as accusations surfaced, he defended her and proclaimed himself as a messenger of God. Both Prophet 'Isa and Maryam (peace be upon them both) are regarded as two of the greatest human beings in our history.

Allah also emphasizes His Mercy throughout this surah. The name "Ar Rahman" is mentioned 13 times in this surah alone, all in the majestic scene. Allah is connecting the possession of power and authority with mercy. We as people attain positions of authority and allow arrogance to bring out the worse of us. Allah is showing that even though He has power over everything in the world, He shows Mercy in all things.

Exercises for Surah Maryam

1. Anytime you engage in dialogue with people of other faiths remember the dialogue between Ja'fir ibn Abi Talib and the king. This was a dialogue of respect, kindness, and understanding.
2. The word, Rahman, is mentioned thirteen times in Surah Maryam. In your interactions with your family members and in interfaith dialogue, put an emphasis on being merciful in dealing with people.
3. The next time that you feel a family member is in the wrong, deal with them with kindness and compassion, as Ibrahim (peace be upon him) was with his father.

Surah Taha (20)

Surah Taha is a Makkan surah that was revealed to the Prophet (peace be upon him) seven years before Hijrah. Surah Taha was the cause of one of the greatest conversions in Islamic history. 'Umar (may Allah be pleased with him) was, at the time, a great enemy of the Prophet Muhammad (peace be upon him). 'Umar had plotted to kill the beloved Messenger and was on his way to execute his plan. He was intercepted before reaching the Prophet (peace be upon him) and informed of the conversion of his own sister. 'Umar immediately redirected himself toward his sister's home, where he found her and her husband reading Qur'an. After an intense confrontation between 'Umar and his sister, he decided to listen to what had so moved his sister and made such a great change in her life. It was this very surah that touched the heart of the man who was known for his hatred of Islam and for the Prophet, along with his inability to control his temper. 'Umar embraced Islam and became one of the greatest supporters, teachers, leaders of Islam, as well as a dear and beloved friend to the Prophet (peace be upon him).

Surah Taha opens with an explanation of what the Qur'an is not; it is not intended to cause distress. Rather, it is intended to bring comfort to the believers and serve as a warning for those who question the words of Allah. It is not meant to limit a person's feeling for this life but to encourage contemplation and understanding of right and wrong. The surah then moves into a long story of Musa (may Allah be pleased with him).

The Surah explains the life and mission of Prophet Musa (peace be upon him). He was born into a time in which the Pharaoh's hatred for the Israelites was so intense that he ordered each male child to be killed. Musa's mother hid her son in order to save him. In verse 38, Allah explains His inspiration to Musa's mother to place her son in a chest and release it into the

89

river as a means for protecting him from harm by the Pharaoh.[49] The chest sailed down the river until it passed in front of the palace. The Pharaoh's people picked it up and the wife of Pharaoh then adopted Musa. In the same verse, Allah indicates that an enemy of Allah would receive Musa, yet Musa's mother believes in Allah and does what He had instructed. Allah grants her the greatest comfort: "But I cast love over you from Me." He recognizes the difficult task He is placing upon the mother of Musa, but what would be greater comfort than knowing that with that task comes a promise of Allah's love? The sister of Musa followed his chest down the river. Upon reaching the palace she suggested to them a woman who would be able to nurse the adopted boy: Musa's own mother. And so Allah reunited young Musa with his mother in Pharaoh's palace. This serves as a reminder to us that in each test, though we may not see it, Allah has a plan and that He never abandons His servants. Allah reiterates this point in verse 46 when Prophet Musa feels anxious and Allah reminds him that he is not alone.

In verses 9-36, Allah tells the story of establishing Musa as a prophet and assigning him his mission. Immediately after Allah declares Himself as the Lord of the Worlds, Allah (swt) tells Musa to establish prayer and to be mindful of the Day of Judgment. Allah shows the importance of prayer in Islam; He declares His Lordship and follows it with the command to pray. We say that we have established Allah as our Lord within our hearts; so then how have so many of us forgotten to establish the very next command? Why is it that Ramadan is the only time that we give our prayers the focus and attention they deserve?

During the initial conversation between Musa (peace be

---

[49]"Behold! We sent to thy mother, by inspiration, the message: 'Throw (the child) into the chest, and throw (the chest) into the river: the river will cast him up on the bank, and he will be taken up by one who is an enemy to Me and an enemy to him': But I cast (the garment of) love over thee from Me: and (this) in order that thou mayest be reared under Mine eye.

upon him) and Allah, Musa (peace be upon him) carries his walking stick. Allah (swt) commands him to throw the stick down; it then turns into a live snake. When he retrieves the snake it returns to its original state as a stick. Not only is Allah showing Musa (peace be upon him) the power that he is being granted as a Prophet of Allah, but Allah is also preparing him for the challenge he will face when he returns to the Pharaoh's palace. Immediately, Allah assigns Prophet Musa (peace be upon him) to go to Pharaoh and tell him of his wrongdoings and invite him to change his ways. Musa (peace be upon him) realizes the difficulty of such a mission and requests the assistance of his brother, Haroon (peace be upon him), which he is granted.

Verses 60-70 explain that when Prophet Musa (peace be upon him) tells Pharaoh of Allah (swt) and his call to worship none other than Him, the Pharaoh accuses him of being a magician and challenges him to show his magic against the Pharaoh's magicians. When they are gathered together the magicians throw their ropes and cause the illusion that the ropes are moving. Prophet Musa then throws his cane, which becomes a snake and devours the ropes. The magicians, knowing well the deception of their tricks, abandon their life of comfort with Pharaoh and immediately prostrate to Allah saying, "We believe in the Lord of Haroon and Musa." We should contemplate the readiness of the magicians to turn to Allah; they witnessed the miracle and they believed. Muslims today have stories upon stories of the miracles of Allah, as well as everyday examples of Allah's greatness. How is it that we are not ready to prostrate as the magicians did even though their lives were threatened? When we know more about Allah than they did, how are we lazy to get to prayer, sometimes abandoning *Fajr* or *Isha* when we are tired, or *Dhuhr* or *'Asr* when it does not fit into our schedules? These sorcerers remind us that the time to submit to Allah is always now as none of us knows if tomorrow will come.

In verse 77, Prophet Musa (peace be upon him) is given the inspiration to flee with his followers from Pharaoh.[50] Allah tells him that Musa (peace be upon) will split the Red Sea in order to save his people. It is in this event that Pharaoh—though he was a king with so much power and wealth—was removed from existence in an instance. Once safe from Pharaoh, Musa (peace be upon him) retreated to the mountain for 40 days and 40 nights. During this time, Allah informed Musa (peace be upon him) of the situation of his people whom he had left under the guidance of the elders and his brother, Haroon (peace be upon him). Prophet Musa (peace be upon him) returned to his people disheartened and found that in his absence they had constructed a calf to worship.

The surah then continues to talk about the Last Day and the two destinations that will accommodate all of humanity. This ties back to the beginning of the surah in which we are informed that the Qur'an was not sent to distress the people. We understand from the descriptions that the Qur'an serves as a warning and a guide so that we can engage in deeds that will bring us closer to the destination we all seek: Paradise.

Exercises for Surah Taha

1. Look at the story of Musa (peace be upon him) and count how many times he was in a difficult situation. Examine how he was relieved of those difficulties and how he handled them.
2. Refrain from judging people. If you find yourself being judgmental, remember how 'Umar (may Allah be pleased with him) made a complete change, from being

---

[50]We sent an inspiration to Moses: "Travel by night with My servants, and strike a dry path for them through the sea, without fear of being overtaken (by Pharaoh) and without (any other) fear."

an enemy of Islam to being one of the greatest Muslim leaders. Allah knows the hearts of people best.

3. Identify experiences in your own life in which you feel you do not have sufficient courage or strength to overcome something. Remind yourself that you are only human and that the right choice, even if it is hard for you, means receiving the love of Allah Almighty.

4. Place prayer on the top of your priority list. When you plan your day, and your family's day, first note the prayer times, and then plan your day around them. Do not allow yourself to plan the other way around.

Surah Al Anbiya (21)

Surah Al Anbiya is a Makkan surah and was amongst the earliest surahs revealed. The surah opens with a reminder of the Day of Reckoning. Allah tells us many times that this Day is promised, it is true, and there is no doubt of its arrival. Surah Al Anbiya also discusses the revelation of the Torah and the Qur'an (verses 48-50). He reminds us that the message conveyed to Musa and Haroon (peace be upon them both) is the same in principle, as that which was sent to Prophet Muhammad (peace be upon him). Both messages differentiate between truth and falsehood, transgressions and righteousness, light and darkness, and fearing and loving Allah. How is it then that we reject what has been conveyed, not only to the final Prophet of Allah, but also to the Prophets generations before him?

While with every moment of our lives we grow closer to the Hour, there are too many of us that disregard it and are careless in our actions. We treat the serious matters of this life without concern and instead direct our attention to the size of the house, the model of the car, the extravagance of the celebrations, and other matters of a trivial nature. Will those things help us on that Day? Allah (swt) reminds us that, though we may preoccupy ourselves with other matters or try to escape the reminder of the *Qiyamah*, there is no place to retreat to except in Allah. Therefore, we must design our actions to relate to things that speak on our behalf rather than against us. Allah (swt) reminds us that He alone is aware of when the Day will come. And as a teacher once reminded us, if you look in the right side mirror of your car you will see written words of caution: "Object is closer than it appears." Similarly, the *Akhirah* is closer to us than it might appear in our minds. We must be cautious of the steps we take as each decision affects our future. While we remind ourselves to correct our mistakes, we should also encourage ourselves to continue the good deeds that we do each day. Even the smallest good deed will be put on our scales and for the righteous Allah has promised the *Akhirah* to be a place of happiness beyond anything we will experience in this world.

Surah Al Anbiya mentions Prophets Lut, Nuh, Dawud, Sulayman, Ayyub, Yunus, Ismail, Yahya, Zakariya, Idris, and 'Isa (peace be upon all of them). This surah speaks a great deal about Prophet Ibrahim (peace be upon him) and in particular his dealings with the idol worshipers. In verses 51-75, Allah (swt) tells us the story of the Prophet known as the friend of Allah, Ibrahim (may Allah be pleased with him). Prophet Ibrahim (peace be upon him) was granted guidance and wisdom from an early age in his life and began calling people to *Tawhid* in his youth. Ibrahim (may Allah be pleased with him) had the task of guiding his people away from falsehood and idol worship, and in doing so he had to confront his father as well. He questioned the actions of his people, and they had nothing greater to justify their actions than that they were following the actions of their fathers before them. This lesson teaches us that we cannot follow our parents, teachers, or Imams blindly. We must internalize what they are giving us, contemplate it and then follow it or leave it based on our thought. The idol worshipers are not free from the sin because they are following the actions of people before them or doing what their fathers did. Those before them will be held accountable and they will be held accountable and one will not be able to protect the other when they come before Allah.

It is important to respect the knowledge that is given to us but we must be a community that is practicing Islam because we understand it and not because another person said "Do" and we react to their command.

Ibrahim (may Allah be pleased with him) tested his people one day by putting their "gods" to a test. The community left for some town festivities and Ibrahim (may Allah be pleased with him) stayed behind. In their absence, he destroyed their idols—all but the biggest one. Immediately upon their return, they questioned Ibrahim as he was the only one left behind capable of such an action. Ibrahim (may Allah be pleased with him) responded to their accusations by suggesting the question be posed to the remaining idol that they prayed to for help on other matters. If the idol was able to provide them with answers before, should it not be able to do so now?

The idol worshipers were confused by Ibrahim's question. All they were able to respond was that Ibrahim knew well that the idols were not capable of such destruction. In their arrogance they refused to see the wisdom behind Prophet Ibrahim's actions. He provided them a great reminder of the limitation of the idols, yet they refused to believe. Rather, they rallied against him and decided to eliminate him by throwing him in a fire. By every law of nature, the fire should have been hot and anyone would have felt the pain of the heat immediately. It is reported by Ibn Abbas that as the Prophet of Allah was being placed into the fire, the angel of rain waited for the command to send down rain as ease for Prophet Ibrahim (peace be upon him). But Allah (swt), as He has told us many times throughout the Qur'an, never abandons His servant. Allah knows the effort that Ibrahim (may Allah be pleased with him) made and the lesson he taught his people (despite their refusal to accept it). He (swt) commanded the fire to be made cool and safe for Prophet Ibrahim (peace be upon him), preventing any harm to him. Allah helps those who are steadfast in His way. "We protect our Prophets and those who believe in this life and in life to come." (Qur'an 40:51) When Ibrahim was asked what the best days of his life were, he replied saying, "The day of the fire," as that was the day he witnessed the greatness of Allah's Mercy.

Allah (swt) then concludes the surah by reminding us of the *Akhirah* and the two destinations. He is calling on us to put our strength toward good deeds while there is still time. All of us will perish and all will be brought in front of Allah for judgment. May Allah purify our actions and cause them to bring us nearer to Him.

Exercises for Surah Al Anbiyah'

1. Make a list of the Prophets of Allah that are mentioned in the Qur'an. Determine a schedule for you or for your family to study the lives of each of these Prophets.
2. As was mentioned earlier in the exercises, do not follow blindly. If you find yourself doing so, remember the story of Ibrahim (May Allah be pleased with him) and his father.
3. Ibrahim (May Allah be pleased with him) said that the day of the fire was one of the greatest days of his life because he witnessed the mercy of Allah (swt) that moment. Do we look for the mercy of Allah in our trials? Next time you are afflicted with a difficulty, look for the good in it and remember that it may not be recognizable immediately. Remind yourself that Allah's wisdom is in all things and He is the greatest of planners.

Surah Al Hajj (22)

Surah Al Hajj is the 22nd surah of the Qur'an. It is not certain if this surah is Makkan of Madinan, but most seem to say it is a Madinan surah. This surah addresses the spiritual aspect of the person, covering faith, belief in the oneness of Allah (swt), the Day of Judgment, the pilgrimage to the Sacred House of Allah (swt), and boundaries upon Muslims engaging in physical combat.

Surah Al Hajj opens with a powerful reminder of the "dramatic convulsion of the Last Hour," the moment in which every person on earth is called to account for the actions of this life. In the second verse, Allah (swt) expresses the shock that we will face at the arrival of the Hour by saying that the nursing mother will forget her child and mankind will be hastening about as if they are intoxicated. The metaphor of the mother abandoning her child is powerful as no mother is able to abandon her child in any amount of danger. Her natural inclination is always to protect her child, but on that Day, a mother does not know her children and children do not know their parents. Each being on earth is left to stand alone before Allah. While those who disobeyed will feel a tremendous fear, the righteous will not feel the same despair and fear. Allah (swt) makes it clear from these verses that, righteous or not, the Hour will be of shock. We will be caught off guard. Therefore, every action of every moment should directed to the way of seeking Allah's pleasure. We never know which action will be our last.

Surah Al Hajj takes its name from verse 27of this surah.[51]It is named after the fifth pillar of Islam, one of the most moving experiences that a Muslim will go through in his or her entire lifetime. Verse 27 calls all of humanity to complete the Hajj, as it is required of every Muslim at least once in their life. It is the journey to Allah's Sacred House. Hajj shows the universality of our beautiful religion. We are one Ummah, one

---

[51]"And proclaim the Pilgrimage among men: they will come to thee on foot and (mounted) on every kind of camel, lean on account of journeys through deep and distant mountain highways;

community, regardless of all of our diversity and any of our differences. Allah (swt) talks about the beauty of Hajj and of witnessing Muslims coming together in masses from all different backgrounds, unifying under the umbrella of belief in Allah (swt) alone and Prophet Muhammad (peace be upon him) as His final Prophet. Each pilgrim is following in the footsteps of our beloved Prophet Ibrahim (may Allah be pleased with him).

In this surah, Allah (swt) connects Hajj with the Day of Judgment. He reminds Muslims that the garment of Hajj is very similar to the garment for the deceased person, also similar to that in which newborn babies are wrapped. Allah (swt) connects Hajj to life's beginning and to its end. Hajj serves as a reminder of Allah's call to us as well as His command for us to seek forgiveness, as death can come at any moment. As the pilgrims stand at the Mount Arafah, everyone is gathered together at one time, pleading to Allah to forgive them. And as they circle the Ka'bah, they announce their response to the call of Allah. Both of these are at times when other options are available to us, and we answer Allah's call and seek His forgiveness by our own will. On the Day of Judgment, we will answer His call regardless of our desire to do so, and the opportunity to ask His forgiveness will be behind us.

Allah (swt) uses the majority of the verses of this surah to emphasize the truth and importance of the Day of Resurrection. Allah (swt) explains in a powerful and humbling explanation in the fifth verse of the surah that the life of this world is nothing more than a test. Allah (swt) gives a detailed description of the creation of each human being and our dependency on Allah (swt) before we are even conscious of our existence in the world. He takes us through the process of coming into being and reminds us that, after birth, it is only a matter of time before we die. How can one not then understand the capability of Allah (swt) to cause something to die and bring it back to life when He is the One capable of creating it and taking life the first time? Allah (swt) knows that the miracle of life is so phenomenal that it in itself may be difficult for us to comprehend, so He provides another analogy. He compares the lifeless earth to earth after He has provided rain to it. We witness this year after year when the seasons change and the trees shed their leaves, then He brings them back to life again after a season of rain and warmth. We see it in summers of drought when the grass becomes brown and crisp and then He brings it back to life. It is a clear sign of Allah's ability to bring life back to what is dead.

Verse 11 talks about those people who are not serious about worshipping Allah (swt), and who want good without trial.[52] They worship Allah (swt) when He is providing for them what they want. But when He withholds something, even if for their own benefit (though they do not know), they abandon their worship. They think they are strong in their faith and that Allah (swt) is in error for not giving them what they are seeking, but Allah (swt) says they are the ones who are in loss of this world and the next world. This is the action of a person who thinks they know more than the Creator. Allah (swt) humbles such people in verses 73 and 74. He challenges us by saying that if we were to all come together for the single purpose of creating a tiny fly, a fly which has the simplest DNA of Allah's creations, we would not succeed. Those who worship Allah (swt) when things are good and leave their worship in times of trial, think they know more than Allah (swt). They think they know what "should have been." Allah (swt) is making the point that He knows the complexities of the world and all of our minds together could not replicate one of His most simple creations.

Surah Al Hajj takes us through one of the greatest acts of *Ibadah*, the Hajj. On the opposite front, He reminds us of one of the most abhorred acts a Muslim can commit, and that is the

---

[52]There are among men some who serve Allah, as it were, on the verge: if good befalls them, they are, therewith, well content; but if a trial comes to them, they turn on their faces: they lose both this world and the Hereafter: that is loss for all to see!

act of unjustly engaging in physical aggression against others. In these verses, Allah (swt) declares permissibility of fighting only in defense and for protecting people from oppression. He (swt) invalidates any other reason for Muslims to engage in war. It is never acceptable to use Islam to initiate war.

Today this verse is very much misinterpreted. The Jihad of the Muslims does not ever involve the taking of innocent life, nor does it allow any room for acts of terrorism. A cornerstone of Muslim belief is fighting injustice, and any person who engages in hostile actions for other than the two reasons mentioned above, has caused a great injustice themselves. Verse 40 continues to discuss the Muslim duty to stand against oppression. It is necessary to stand up and advocate for the weak, and be the voice of the voiceless.

Throughout Surah Al Hajj, Allah (swt) reminds us of the rewards of those who follow His path and the punishments of those who choose to go astray. May Allah (swt) grant us the opportunity to visit His Sacred House, to be people of righteousness, justice and peace, and may He grant us *Jannatul Firdous*.

Exercises for Surah Hajj

1. If you have not gone for Hajj, think about what is stopping you from going this year? If you have the means, do not delay. If you cannot go this year, start planning your life around how you can save the means to get there, rather than spending on extra things and waiting until the money adds up on its own.
2. Personalize the Day of Judgment. Small events happen in your life that shake you; imagine how that Day will shake you.
3. Pick a place in nature with which you and your family are familiar. This can be your backyard, a park, a

vacation place, etc. Take a picture of the area in the summer when everything is green and alive. Take a second picture in the winter of the same trees that are lifeless or covered with ice and snow. Keep these pictures in your house as a reminder of Allah's ability to bring back to life that which is dead. Share them with your children and talk about the changes of seasons being a sign from Allah of the resurrection.

4. Do your research on the "touchy" topics. The words 'terrorism', 'violence', and *'jihad'* are being used by some people almost interchangeably. Use the Qur'anic verses on *Jihad*, in their correct context, to understand their true meaning. And speak up when you hear people use the word *"jihad"* to justify forbidden acts of violence and terrorism.

Surah Al Mu'minun (23)

Surah Al Mu'minun is a Makkan surah that discusses virtues that are the foundation of faith. Allah (swt) describes true believers as those who implement these virtues in all aspects of life. Allah (swt) reminds us that success is not based on material wealth or status, but rather on dedication to our faith.

The second verse of this surah talks about those who humble themselves in their prayer. So how can we attain further concentration and humility in prayer? We must first understand the importance of the prayer itself.

As we read in Surah Taha, Allah (swt) commands the establishment of prayer after He commands the establishment of belief in Him. Likewise, He mentions *Salah* on the top of a list of actions that make a person successful in His eyes. Before we begin to pray, we must recognize before whom we are standing when we pray. While this is something that may be difficult, as our minds are not capable of fully comprehending all the attributes of Allah (swt), we can begin by learning, memorizing, and internalizing the meanings of what we aresaying in prayer. Once we know them and understand them, we can recite them with the conviction they deserve. Surah Fatiha is something that we recite in every *rakah* of every prayer; do we take time in our *salah* to really think about the meaning? This surah is unique in the sense that it is a conversation between Allah and His servant. For each verse we recite, Allah responds to our supplication. Allah (swt) has commanded His servants to bow down to Him by placing a person's most beloved feature—the face—on the ground. This position is spiritually beneficial for the servant as it humbles him and reminds him where he came from and where he will return.

The word *"Salah"* comes from "Sil," or "to connect." It is the direct line of communication between Allah (swt) and us. We must understand that with each prayer we are able to open our hearts to our Creator, to confide our difficulties, to express our gratitude, to seek His forgiveness, and to appeal for His guidance. Prayer should become routine in the sense of regularity but prayer should never become routine spiritually. Prayer is a powerful connection and we must eliminate internal and external distractions in order to make the best connection. This means that while we must not scold our children for being fidgety in prayer, we must also not allow them to run and scream. We should try to minimize excessive movement. And we must remember to silence our electronic reminders of the *Dunya* that distract us from the *Akhirah* and our conversation with our Lord.

Prayer serves as a unifier for Muslims as well. The congregational prayer brings Muslims together, reminding us that Muslims are supposed to act as a source of strength for each other, and that we cannot live our lives isolated from everyone else. In congregational prayer we are encouraged to pray shoulder to shoulder. The Prophet Muhammad (peace be upon him) did not ask the poor to stand in the back rows of *salah*, or the Arabs to pray closest to the Imam. He taught us to stand side by side, emphasizing the equality of humanity. It unites Muslims of various backgrounds by their shared love of Allah (swt). It is, however, the responsibility of the knowledgeable to stand near the Imam in order to correct him if he makes any mistake. The congregational prayer brings Muslims of every nationality, ethnicity, and race together. It is a reminder that we cannot allow those things to divide us as on the Day of Judgment we will all be called together as one group; humanity.

Salah also teaches us the importance of respecting time. The prayers are spread throughout the day and into the night. Just as we use the sun and the moon to calculate the passing of the days, the daily completion of the five prayers reminds our souls of the passing of time and nearness of the *Qiyamah*. It is vital that we make prayer a priority in our lives. For those of us who are uncertain about our commitment to our prayers, we should ask ourselves if we plan our day around our *salah* or our *salah* around our day. If we are doing the latter, we must evaluate our priorities and make the necessary changes.

Allah (swt) also reminds us of other traits while He defines as those that lead to success. He mentions the importance of paying the *Zakah*, and fulfilling our promises to protect our health, wealth, children, and the earth that He has blessed us with. Allah (swt) commands us to guard against sin and perversion. We must recognize what Allah (swt) has forbidden for us altogether and what He has made permissible for us with conditions and limitations. In the current state of the world we live in, this is important for everyone to be mindful of, most especially our youth. The world is inviting you to good and bad; you must use the wisdom Allah (swt) has blessed you with and the guidance He has provided you to make sound decisions that will lead you, and keep you on His path.

Allah (swt) gives us the examples of the Prophet Nuh and Prophet Musa (peace be upon them both) in this surah. He shows us how they lived these virtues and, though their people challenged them, they were successful in the eyes of Allah (swt). Allah (swt) refers to the characteristics of the *Mu'minun* in this surah. He reminds us in verse 115: "Did ye then think that We had created you in jest, and that ye would not be brought back to Us for account?" Let us contemplate and evaluate ourselves against these virtues in our lives. Allah has given us the elements to become successful. May He help us to try to adhere to them before we are questioned regarding them.

Exercises for Surah Al Mu'minun

1. "The believers will eventually be successful through…" (23:1) Write down the actions that follow this verse. Where do you match up against these?
2. Take your time when you make *wudu*.
3. Allow yourself plenty of time for prayer; do not rush your conversation with your Creator. Put Allah (swt) above and before everything else.
4. Learn the meanings of what you are saying in your prayer.
5. Turn your cell phone and all other distractions off before you pray.
6. Stop backbiting. Unfortunately, it is an easy habit to pick up, but it is also a very easy habit to break. If you find yourself in a group where others are backbiting, change the conversation to something permissible. If that does not work, excuse yourself from the group.
7. Everyone wants money. Make a list of the things you make sure you do every day in order to put money in your bank (you get up early, wear you best clothes, work hard at work, you do everything your boss asks of you to keep him happy, etc). Now make a list of what you do, or what you want to try to do, every day to deposit Allah's pleasure in your "*akhirah* account". Both

accounts are important, do not be neglectful of them and always remember the latter is more important.

Surah An Nur (24)

Surah An Nur is the 24th surah in the Qur'an. It is a Madinan surah that was revealed near the end of the fifth or the beginning of the sixth year of Hijrah. The content of the surah deals with aspects of Islamic law and the organization of a moral social society. It particularly addresses protection of family and community relationships and includes the incident that happened with Aisha (may Allah be pleased with her), and the false accusations made against her.

Verses 1-31 address the social issues of Muslims as they make transition out of the *Jahiliya* period into the light of Islam. Allah (swt) opens the surah by establishing the importance of protecting the decency and modesty of the Muslims in society. He describes the various situations of accusations made against others, laying out the consequences for each, including the accuser if they cannot bring all four witnesses to support their accusation. Allah (swt) has set guidelines for us to protect society and bring and maintain social order.

In verses 21 and 22, Allah (swt) reminds us that Shaytan has vowed to call us to sin and wrongdoing. The historical context of this verse reminds Muslims that it is never acceptable to respond to injustice with injustice. If we do not remain steadfast in the face of trial, Shaytan takes advantage of our weakened state and tries to call us to respond in any way that is displeasing to Allah (swt).

Shaytan tries to lead us in steps. This verse was in reference to the father of Aisha, Abu Bakr (may Allah be pleased with them both). His own cousin, whom he supported out of his kindness, was amongst those making accusations against Aisha. Abu Bakr desired to withhold his support to his cousin as penance for his lies. But Abu Bakr (may Allah be pleased with him) was a man of such character that he chose to show kindness rather than anger. Allah (swt) is always forgiving of His servant—should we not attempt to do the same?

Surah An Nur also discusses the issues of privacy and modesty. In verses 27 and 28, Allah (swt) explains the appropriate Islamic etiquette upon entering another's property. He reminds us to seek permission and exchange greetings. If a person is denied permission, or if a house is vacant at the time, they should leave gracefully, without any resentment. Verses 30 and 31 then talk about modesty. This is something extremely important for Muslims today to keep in mind in all interactions. Similar to what we read above, Allah (swt) places punishment suitable for the crime. Similarly, He recognizes the weaknesses of His creations and places the necessary restrictions to maintain balance and protection.

Allah (swt) declares the limitations of the gaze (particularly for men), and the guarding of modesty (particularly for women, except in front of certain male relatives). Allah uses the Arabic word "Khimar," a veil, covering her head and chest. Unfortunately today we see many people struggle with this command of Allah (swt). It is important for us to remember that Allah (swt) did not decree things because they are easy. He did so because He knows these things to be good for us as individuals and as a community. If you find any command of Allah (swt) to be a struggle, do not abandon it, but work harder to fulfill it and Allah (swt) will multiply the reward for your effort.

Verse 35 uses the metaphor of a light. The light is the spark for the spiritual flame in the heart of the believer.[53] The oil

---

[53]Allah is the Light of the heavens and the earth. The Parable of His Light is as if there were a Niche and within it a Lamp: the Lamp enclosed in Glass: the glass as it were a brilliant star: Lit from a blessed Tree, an Olive, neither of the east nor of the west, whose oil is

that keeps it burning is the righteous deeds we engage in and our acts of worship. The oil comes from a blessed tree that is the Qur'an and our belief in Allah (swt) alone. But like any flame, it needs to be protected from the wind. The wind in this metaphor is the sin we commit that takes life out of the spirit. But we must not lose hope if the light becomes weak; the flame regains its strength through continuing good deeds. Over time, the glass around the light may become darkened by smoke, but cleaning the heart is like cleaning the glass, and once it has been cleaned, the light will shine through again.

In contrast, the state of those who reject faith is like that of a person in the middle of the dark deep ocean. The dark and stormy waves prevent them from even seeing their own outstretched hand. They are lost in the depths of darkness without any light to guide them. They reject the light of the Qur'an that Allah (swt) offered to them and, as a result, they do not know who they are.

Allah (swt) ends this surah with a strong message to all of humanity: "They swear their strongest oaths by Allah (swt) that, if only thou wouldst command them, they would leave (their homes). Say: "Swear ye not: Obedience is more reasonable; Verily, Allah is well acquainted with all that you do." Allah (swt) is telling us in this verse that it does not suffice to say, "We believe in Allah," but that we have to back these words with our actions. We say that we are committing ourselves to Allah (swt), but if we do not obey His commands or we abandon what He forbids, are we truly believing in Him? We must work hard to make Islam a religion that we live, not just that we proclaim.

---

well-nigh luminous, though fire scarce touched it: Light upon Light! Allah doth guide whom He will to His Light: Allah doth set forth Parables for men: and Allah doth know all things.

---

1. Look at the callings of Allah (swt) in this surah (the verses starting with "O you who believe" or "O you people"). Identify your areas of weakness related to these callings and document what steps you will take to respond to His call or His command.

2. When you hear a rumor or accusation about someone, do not spread it or add to it. Imagine if you were in that person's shoes. Stop and assess if the matter is concerning you; if so, verify it before acting. If it is not concerning you, ignore it.

3. Evaluate if you are doing things in your everyday life that are protecting your spiritual flame from the wind. How often are you taking the time to clean the smoky glass around your heart?

Surah Al Furqan (25)

Surah Al Furqan is a Makkan surah and the 25th in the order of compilation. *Furqan* is the "Criterion'" or the "Standard of True and False." It is also another name for the Book of Allah (swt), as every believer should use its words as a measurement of where we stand in the eyes of Allah (swt).

Allah (swt) opens Surah Al Furqan by mentioning the disbelievers and those that mocked the Prophets of Allah (swt). In verses 11-16, Allah (swt) gives an intense reminder of both the Hellfire and Paradise. Those who deny the Day of Judgment are reminded of the fury of the Fire that they can hear even before they are close enough to see it. The Fire is described as being angry and hungry, as if waiting for the fuel that keeps it going, man and stone. The sounds of Hellfire will put such fear in the hearts of the wrongdoers that they will plead to be obliterated from existence, but all they ask for at that point is of no use. They let the time for forgiveness and change pass in their life on earth.

Allah (swt) then describes Paradise as a place that is greater than anything on earth and where every wish will be granted. Who can turn away such an offer? Allah (swt) is saying that everything that we ever wished for is attainable if we live this life in a righteous and obedient way. Allah (swt) then poses the question of what the person prefers: the anguish of the Fire that is beyond comprehension, or the bliss of Paradise that is perfect and eternal? Allah (swt) is reminding us that while Shaytan is present and always trying to deter us from good, the choice and the accountability is ours in the end.

The deniers of the Qur'an are determined to question Allah (swt), His Messengers, and His Book. In the previous surah, we saw that they mocked the Prophets of Allah (swt) about being nothing more than human beings. And as we have read in and understood from previous surahs, this is in fact one of the great blessings, as it allows people to relate to their situations and believe they can also attain nearness to Allah (swt). Similarly, the disbelievers mocked the fact that the revelation of the Qur'an is in phases, but this too is a blessing. Some of the practices and customs of the *Jahiliya* Arabs were every far from the boundaries of Islam. To have revealed the Qur'an all at once may have been overwhelming for the people and may have prevented them from making the transition into the laws of Islam. This is a lesson for us as well, that when we engage in dialogue with other Muslims or non-Muslims, we must not force Islam onto them. Allah (swt) brought Islam to the people over the course of 23 years. We cannot ask a person who just entered Islam to absorb 23 years of commands overnight. Allah (swt) shows us that it is okay to take time to progress forward in your *Iman*. Small steps that remain consistent are better than leaps that you cannot nurture and sustain.

In verse 43, Allah (swt) draws our attention to our own

desires to overrule His command.[54] Allah (swt) is telling the Prophet (peace be upon him) that there are some who will never be guided. Those who follow their desires without concern for the commands of Allah (swt) are among those people. They are compared to cattle that do what they are created to do; yet these people go against their purpose in life and do not give a second thought to it. Such people Allah (swt) describes as never being guided have never seen and will never see the light of Allah (swt). At the same time, there are those amongst us who have been given the light of Allah (swt) but fall into error. And Allah (swt) reminds us in verses 70 and 71, that as long as we ask Allah (swt) for His forgiveness, He will forgive. Even if we have transgressed into deep crimes, the door to Allah's forgiveness is always open and if we seek it with sincerity, then Allah (swt) can change our evil habits into good habits.

Allah (swt) describes in verse 63 the beautiful characteristics of the people who have taken the Criterion in their life and have earned the title of the "Servant of the Merciful."[55] Let us measure ourselves against the descriptions of these verses and see where we stand.

"O Allah grant us spouses and offspring that will be the comfort of our eyes, and give us the grace to lead the righteous," (25:74).

Exercises for Surah Al Furqan

1. Use the descriptions of Heaven and Hell as motivators and deterrents for you. Compile the descriptions of

---

[54]"Seest thou such a one as taketh for his god his own passion (or impulse)? Couldst thou be a disposer of affairs for him?
[55]"And the servants of (Allah) Most Gracious are those who walk on the earth in humility, and when the ignorant address them, they say, "Peace!";

these two that you read throughout the Qur'an and return to them as often as you need.

2. Be patient with yourself as you strive to be better. Plan small but consistent changes, rather than large unsustainable ones.

    a. If you are not praying all of your five required prayers start there. Remember that it is absolutely never too late to turn to Allah and ask forgiveness for your mistakes.

    b. If you ever feel like you cannot approach prayer or make *dua* because of past transgressions, take the time to sit down before you pray and say *"Astaghfirullah"* twenty, fifty, or a hundred times. While it is not required it will help you connect with your Lord in prayer rather than feel distant. Remember all humans make mistakes and He is always listening and ready to forgive.

    c. If you are praying all your required prayers, establish the habit of praying at night. You do not have to start praying twenty *rakat* every night, just start with 2 *rakah* before Fajr prayer, once a month. If you are married, do this together with your spouse. It will benefit your relationship with Allah and with each other.

3. Learn the *dua* 25:74 and repeat it often.

Surah Ash Shu'ara (26)

Surah Ash Shu'ara is a Makkan surah that was revealed to the Prophet (peace be upon him) at a time when he had begun to feel disappointment in the pagans' lack of interest in Islam. In fact, with each step that he tried to take forward in preaching, the pagans pushed back that much more. They continued this until they became fond of witnessing the distress of the beloved Prophet of Allah (swt) and his followers. The first few verses of the surah serve as a source of comfort to the Muslims. They

111

reassure them that the Book of Allah is the Truth and that it is Allah who will resolves matters with those who reject faith.

Allah (swt) reminds Prophet Muhammad (peace be upon him) of the struggles of the prophets that came before him. In verse 10, He begins the story of Musa (peace be upon him) who had great hesitation about going to Pharaoh alone and about calling him to the path of Allah (swt). He asked for a partner and was granted his brother, Haroon (peace be upon him). Allah (swt) reminds Prophet Muhammad (peace be upon him) of the fear Musa (peace be upon him) felt and Allah (swt) responded to Musa by saying, "We are with you and We listen to your call." This should be a reminder to all of us as well—that Allah (swt) does not abandon the servant who follows His command. Though we do not hear it directly from Him, we must keep that knowledge in our hearts.

Allah (swt) also gives us the reminder of Prophet Ibrahim's struggle to call his people to Islam. The story of Prophet Ibrahim (peace be upon him) was one that Allah commanded Prophet Muhammad to recite to his *Ummah*, encouraging them to practice the same sincerity towards Allah (swt) and worship none other than Him. Prophet Ibrahim (peace be upon him) voiced his dislike of the idols publicly. He did not concern himself with how his people would react. In verses 77-89, Prophet Ibrahim (peace be upon him) tells his people of the greatness of Allah (swt). Is there someone that we depend on for these things other than Allah (swt)? Each day of our lives, we should contemplate and thank Allah (swt) for His guidance, for food and drink, for cures from our illnesses, and for His willingness to forgive.

In verses 83-89, Prophet Ibrahim (peace be upon him) made *du'a* for himself and for his father, an idol worshiper. Though his father had rejected the foundations of Prophet Ibrahim's belief, Prophet Ibrahim (peace be upon him) was still kind and gentle with him. We should remember this in all of our interactions; though we may not agree, we must speak with others in a kind and respectful manner. Allah (swt) also provides similar examples from the stories of Nuh, Lut and the people of 'Ad and Thamud.

The name "Shu'ara" means "poets." This surah was revealed in a place where poetry was an art and a favorite pastime. The Muslims abandoned much of the poetry as it contradicted the principles of the Islamic faith, sometimes promoting violence or degrading women. This type of entertainment is poison to the heart.

However, for the poetry that complimented the Islamic principles, Muslims enjoyed joining in. The Prophet (peace be upon him) himself took part in these gatherings. This shows us that the Muslims enjoyed poetry as a way of promoting the principles and values of the religion. We should take from this the lesson that it is permissible to use various avenues of entertainment to promote positive values and morals. We must be very cautious to not allow these forms of media to be a source of engaging in anything that is displeasing to Allah (swt). This is especially important for our youth and children as their environment more easily influences them. It is important to remember that what comes out of a person is a representation of what is in their heart, but the heart is only changed by what is put inside of it.

O our Lord! Bestow wisdom on us and join us with the righteous and make us among the inheritors of the Garden of Bliss.

Exercises for Surah Ash Shu'ara

---

1. Allah (swt) is the one who cures all illnesses. If you are ill or hurt, put your hand on the place of the pain or

illness and say the following supplication: "I ask Allah the Lord of the Mighty Throne to heal me."

2. Enjoy entertainment but be mindful that it should be something that promotes the principles and values of Islam in its content and in its delivery. If you have children, pay particular attention to this in regards to their choice of entertainment.

3. Learn the following *dua*: "O our Lord! Bestow wisdom on me and join me with the righteous and make me among the inheritors of the Garden of Bliss."

Surah An Naml (27)

Surah An Naml is the 27th surah in the Qur'an and was revealed in the Makkan period. In this surah Allah (swt) tells us the story of Prophet Sulayman, the son of Prophet Dawud (may Allah be pleased with them both). He explains the power and authority that was granted to Prophet Sulayman (peace be upon him) in this world. He was granted the exceptional power over Mankind and Jinns. He was also granted the talent of understanding the language of the animals. Prophet Sulayman (peace be upon him) not only inherited prophethood, but kingship as well. This is not to say that prophethood is inherited by lineage, but in this case, it was a father and son.

Prophet Sulayman (peace be upon him) and his men happened upon a gathering of ants. One of the ants heard them and warned the others to return to their habitation for safety. Prophet Sulayman (peace be upon him), with his unique gift, was able to understand their communication and said, "O my Lord! So order me that I may be grateful for Your favors, which You have bestowed upon me and on my parents, and that I work righteousness that will please You."

While this story involves one of the tiniest of creations, there is a great lesson to be learned in it. Allah (swt) is showing us a powerful and wealthy leader who is humbled by Allah's creation, regardless of its position in this world. In the eyes of Allah (swt), that creature has spent its entire day and night in worship, doing exactly what Allah (swt) has commanded. What, then, makes us—a creature capable of error in any speech, thought, or action—better than the ant? We feel superior to them, but from what perspective? Prophet Sulayman (peace be upon him) recognizes the beauty of this gift from Allah (swt) and immediately asks Him to make him grateful for it and to use it in a way that will be pleasing to Him. Is this how we react to the gifts Allah (swt) gives us? When we get food at the end of the day, a check at the end of the month, our health, or our intellect, do we respond with gratitude, or do we credit it to our own efforts?

Let us reflect on verses 59-64 of Surah An Naml:

"Say: Praise be to Allah, and Peace on His servants whom He has chosen (for his Message). (Who) is better: Allah or the false gods they associate (with Him)?

"Or, Who has created the heavens and the earth, and Who sends you down rain from the sky? Yea, with it We cause to grow well-planted orchards full of beauty of delight: it is not in your power to cause the growth of the trees in them. (Can there be another) god besides Allah. Nay, they are a people who swerve from justice.

"Or, Who has made the earth firm to live in; made rivers in its midst; set thereon mountains immovable; and made a separating bar between the two bodies of flowing water? (Can there be another) god besides Allah. Nay, most of them know not.

"Or, Who listens to the (soul) distressed when it calls on Him, and Who relieves it's suffering, and makes you (mankind) inheritors of the earth? (Can there be another) god besides Allah. Little it is that ye heed!

"Or, Who guides you through the depths of darkness on land and sea, and Who sends the winds as heralds of glad tidings, going before His Mercy? (Can there be another) god besides Allah? High is Allah above what they associate with Him!

"Or, Who originates creation, then repeats it, and who gives you sustenance from heaven and earth? (Can there be another) god besides Allah. Say, 'Bring forth your argument, if ye are telling the truth!'"

The order of these verses causes us to reflect on those things that we have taken for granted. They reinforce the Majesty of Allah (swt).

Exercises for Surah An Naml

1. Recognize the gifts that Allah (swt) has given us, as Prophet Sulayman did. Show gratitude for them.
    a. When we recognize those blessings, find the way to use each of those things as means for attaining Allah's pleasure.
    b. Be appreciative for Allah's creation by preventing harm. Conserve water and protect animals, trees, plants and the rights and well-being of people.
2. Evaluate your relationship with people. Change your attitude if you belittle others as Allah (swt) tells us that He is the only one who can judge between us.
3. If others belittle you, or in any other time of trial, remember the *dua* from the story of Nuh (peace be upon him), "O Allah I feel helpless, bestow your help upon me."

6

Surah Al Qasas to Surah Ghafir

Surah Al Qasas (28)

Surah Al Qasas is the 28th surah of the Qur'an, revealed in the Makkan period. The surah emphasizes the troubles of those that reject the faith as well as the reward for those who do good and follow in Allah's path.

Surah Al Qasas talks about the story of Musa (peace be upon him).In this story we learn of the great presence of women in the life of Musa, as well as the arrogance of the dictatorship of Pharaoh.

The first woman in his life was his mother. Allah (swt) reminds us of the great test she was made to face when the oppressive Pharaoh ordered midwives to kill all Israelite male children. She hid her son and cared for him herself. And when Allah (swt) asked her to release him into the river for his safety, she obeyed. Except for her deep trust in Allah (swt), she had no assurance of being reunited with her son. Allah (swt) rewarded her for her patience and reunited her with Musa (peace be upon him) and allowed her to help raise him.

The second women, described in verse 11, in the life of Musa (peace be upon him) was his sister, who followed him down the river and negotiated bringing to the palace a woman (his mother) who could nurse young Musa (peace be upon him).[56] In verses 8 and 9, Allah also mentions the wife of Pharaoh who adopts the child and brings him up as a pious

---

[56]And she said to the sister of (Moses), "Follow him" so she (the sister) watched him in the character of a stranger. And they knew not.

person, despite the influence Pharaoh may have had on those around him.

Allah (swt) also mentions the two daughters of Shuayb (peace be upon him) and how, through helping them, Musa (peace be upon him) found his livelihood and a spouse, as one of the two later became Prophet Musa's wife. Here we learn about interaction between Musa (peace be upon him) and the daughters of Shuayb (peace be upon him). This provides us with an example of appropriate gender interaction.

This story of Musa (peace be upon him) also emphasizes the extreme oppression of Pharaoh and how Allah (swt) blesses those who work in His way. Musa (peace be upon him) was raised in the palace of Pharaoh and was no doubt encouraged to feel superior to others. Yet Allah (swt) gave him prophethood, commanded him to confront Pharaoh and enabled him to be successful. Pharaoh's transgressions against other human beings led to his destruction in this life and turned him into a symbol of oppression throughout the history of mankind. Allah (swt) promises that those who oppress others will feel the punishment of it in this life and the hereafter.

Surah Al Qasas also talks about Qarun. Qarun was a man of extreme wealth and power, who fascinated people because of these two things. Qarun did not attribute his success to Allah (swt), where it belonged, but rather arrogantly claimed to be responsible for attaining his wealth and power.

We see similar conduct today. We must always remember that there is nothing on this earth that we can see or not see, touch or not touch, that has not been the result of Allah's decree. Each penny is from Him (swt) and we must remember to be humble and grateful for it. Qarun was not, and so as easily as Allah (swt) gave it to him, He was able to take it away. As Allah (swt) explains in verses 79 and 80, some held Qarun in great esteem merely for his wealth and power, while others recognized the test of wealth and power that Allah (swt) had placed on Qarun. They remembered that the reward of the Hereafter is greater than any reward in this life. These stories teach us morals and virtues. It is important to seek lessons from such stories; Allah (swt) never tells a story only for entertainment.

May Allah make us among those who recognize the test of Allah, and remember that this life is only a temporary abode.

Exercises for Surah Al Qasas

---

1. When looking for a spouse, for yourself or for your children, look at their *iman*. Do not make a judgment based on their resume. Do not be a hurdle for your children if they select based on *iman* above personal preferences that you may have. Refer back to the story of Shuayb if you find yourself in this situation.
2. Similarly, when options come before you, do not pick worldly things above principles. Evaluate your method of decision making for things that have spiritual benefits and costs and things that have material benefits and costs.
3. When you are blessed with something, more money, increased health, etc., make sure that you show gratitude to Allah (swt) and do not attribute credit only to yourself.

Surah Al Ankabut (29)

Surah Al Ankabut is the twenty-ninth surah of the Qur'an and was revealed in the Makkan period. Surah Al Ankabut focuses on belief being tested by trials.

This surah begins with a powerful verse questioning man if he really thinks that he will be left alone in this world without any test. Allah (swt) has already promised that the faith of each person will be tested with trial. We will be tested by removal of things: health, status, and material objects; and we will be tested by being granted things: children, knowledge, wealth, and authority. It is how we respond to that trial that determines our status with Allah (swt) and our destination in the life to come.

Allah (swt) gives us another beautiful metaphor in verse 41, "The parable of those who take protectors other than Allah is that of the spider, who builds to itself a house; but truly the flimsiest of houses is the spider's house if they but knew". When the spider constructs its web, it believes it to be very strong, but from the perspective of the human, the spider's web is flimsy and can easily be wiped away. Even the strongest of webs can be removed in an instance. Similarly, man builds his life on earth in a way that he thinks it will last forever. But this life is just a brief moment in time. Allah's plan and power are far greater than ours. Allah (swt) is drawing the example of the flimsy web to that of the people who worship and rely on things other than Allah (swt). They seek money, knowledge, and physical strength to make themselves successful, but they are just relaying on the strength of that little web. Allah (swt) explained to us in Surah Al Mu'minun, the true meaning and methods for success and it is those who adhere to that plan who will build a solid home in Paradise.

In verse 38 and 40 Allah (swt) gives us the examples of the people of 'Ad and Thamud, and the example of Qarun. These were the people and nations of great power and status but Allah destroyed them by different means as quickly as the hand destroys the web. They built their lives off of something that was not sustainable; they did not build it out of fear and love for Allah (swt).

Allah (swt) reminds us that every soul will taste death. This is a universal fact that no person can escape. This life is only a short life and is nothing more than a life of tests; the *real* life is the life to come. We are on a journey to a final destination. What deeds will we collect in order to attain permission to enter Paradise?

Exercises for Surah Al Ankabut

---

1. Study the concept of *"fitnah"*. Fitnah specifically comes from a test that someone goes through (a trial or a hardship); this includes money and children. Look at every calamity or problem in your life, and look at the benefit that comes out of it. First thank Allah (swt) that the test is not in your faith, and that the calamity is not more severe, and know in your heart that Allah (swt) will compensate you for it.
2. In times of test, if you ever ask yourself "Why me?" you are thinking about the "you" of this world. Consider the "you" of the afterlife. The more you are tested and are patient, the more you are gaining for yourself in the Hereafter.
3. A spider can weave a web that can be wiped away in a moment. But the spider can easily weave a new web elsewhere because it has a skill that comes from within that no one can touch. Humans can build a house, and it can be destroyed in a moment by any natural disaster, or emptied by robbers. If we build our lives only on material things in our home, when they are lost we have lost every thing. If we build the foundation of our family's home on love and fear of Allah, then we realize that while we have lost things, they were *only* things.

Surah Ar Rum (30)

The beginning verses were sent down in regards to the victory over the king of Persia. This shows the great power of the Qur'an as it was telling the Arabs of what happened in the past and what would happen in the future.

In verse 9 of Surah Ar Rum, Allah (swt) reminds Muslims that no generation is better than the one before it except in moral values.[57] He tells us to contemplate on the stories of previous civilizations and see the ruin that came upon them as a result of their deviations and arrogance. We should reflect on the punishment they received in order to appreciate the true Might of Allah. Though they were powerful and held positions of status, they did not have what sustains a community: moral values and *Tawhid*.

In verses 20-22, Allah (swt) reminds us of some of His greatest signs. He reminds us of our creation from mere dust into humans scattered all around the world into various colors, languages, customs, and generations. Though we all came from a single pair of parents, we have been spread to all corners of the earth as various types of people. Yet the common factor remains that we are all dependent on Allah (swt). This verse makes it clear that, in Islam, there is no place for racism.

Allah (swt) is calling us to celebrate our diversity in order to enrich the human experience. Allah (swt) created diversity by design. If we truly understood and appreciated it, we would not see *Masajid* divided on cultural lines, and we would not see segregation based on class, and ethnic wars taking place all around the world. If we truly appreciated the gift of diversity, we would eradicate the world of prejudices. This is one of the beauties of a diverse community. If we take the opportunity to appreciate each other's differences, rather than distance ourselves as result of them, and to embrace our

---

[57]Do they not travel through the earth, and see what was the end of those before them? They were superior to them in strength: they tilled the soil and populated it in greater numbers than these have done: there came to them their apostles with Clear (Signs). (Which they rejected, to their own destruction): It was not Allah Who wronged them, but they wronged their own souls.

similarities, rather than embrace the desire to feel superior, we will be a blessed community that will be successful in this world, and *Insha'Allah* in the life to come. We should all recognize this challenge and humble ourselves amongst our brothers and sisters, remembering that there is nothing that makes one of us better than the other in the sight of Allah (swt), except righteousness and *Taqwa*.

Allah (swt) also mentions another of His signs that is crucial to the success of our community, explained in verse 21: "And among His signs is this, that He has created for you mates from among yourselves, that ye may dwell in tranquility with them. And He has put love and mercy between your hearts. Verily in that are signs for those who reflect." This verse talks about the beginning of a family, the foundation of the Islamic community. Allah is reminding us that this is a sacred relationship that is built on mutual love and respect. Like all good in the world, the relationship of marriage and the bonds of a family require effort and patience. Allah (swt) uses the word *"muwada,"* meaning "an active love that requires effort." There is no room for selfishness within such relationship. When two people make a commitment to each other they are changing the focus of their life from the singular to the plural and making a contract before Allah (swt) to adhere to His laws in regard to caring for each other and bringing each other closer to Him.

Allah (swt) also uses the word *"sakina,"* tranquility, in verse 21. *Sakina* comes from *"saakin,"* the place where you live. Therefore, we understand from this verse that the husband, the wife, and the family that they establish should live in a home that brings them tranquility. It should be a place of kind speech; a place of forgiveness and understanding; a place where persons can be themselves without fear of any harm or hurt; and a place of emotional comfort. Going back to the understanding of verse 21, if we exhibit the same understanding and appreciation within our families that we see explained in this verse, then we will be able to attain that tranquility.

In the last verse of Surah Ar Rum, Allah (swt) reminds us that whatever we face in this world requires patient perseverance. As we strive to improve our relationships with those around us we must remember that even steps towards good, and good itself, can be a test. The beloved Prophet Muhammad (peace be upon him) stood firm in his faith through all tests that Allah (swt) placed before him, because Allah (swt) promised to be on the side of those who are patient. Who better to have on our side, then the Lord of the Universe?

Let us seek to strengthen our families, our communities, and meet the difficult situations being faced by so many people around the world, with the patience and perseverance modeled by our beloved Prophet Muhammad (peace be upon him).

Exercises for Surah Ar Rum

1. Appreciate the diversity of people and languages that are around you. This month get to know a Muslim from another background and culture than your own. And as you look for the similarities that help you build your friendship, remember that the differences are a sign from Allah (swt).
2. Do something consistently for a few months for people of a country other than your own.
3. Take an active role in making sure your *masjid* and community are being a model example of eradicating racism.
4. Practice *Muwadda* in all aspects of your life, starting with your parents, spouse, and children. Look at your marriage and see if it has tranquility, mercy, and compassion.
5. Do not take any relationship for granted. Practice active love, by letting those around you know that you care.

Surah Luqman (31)

Luqman was known to be a man of great intelligence—"Luqman al Hakeem." He was wise in his knowledge of Allah (swt) and the world around him but he was also wise in his dealings with others and in his work.

In verse 12 of Surah Luqman, we read about a dialogue that he is having with his son. We see from this the importance of engaging in dialogue with our children and our youth. It is necessary for parents to recognize that talking to their children will help them make the right decisions. At times parents feel frustrated with what seems like their children's disinterest in what parents are saying, so we unknowingly reserve our communication for times of great stress. Children absorb what is in the world around them, often times much more quickly than we think. If we continue to encourage them and remind them of what is pleasing to Allah (swt), they will absorb that and, as a result, they will make the right decisions and learn to counter negative peer pressure.

What should also be noted is the gentle nature in which Luqman is speaking to his son, "Ya Bunay," "O my beloved son." Is this how we address our children when we speak with them, with such kind and gentle words? It is only natural that if we extend such love, their hearts will open to what we have to say. Therefore, we must look beyond the mistakes that we see them make so that we can constantly and consistently engage in communication that expresses our desire to see them attain the best in this life and the next life.

Unfortunately, the current state of the society that our children are growing up in is contradictory to some core values of Islam. Luqman, in his dialogue with his son is not discussing the most detailed topics in Islam. He is reminding his son of the foundaional belief of our faith: "O my son! Join not in worship others with Allah." Therefore, while it may seem to us like common sense to avoid dressing in a manner as is standard in the society today, or that drugs are bad for a person's health and spirit, these are the greatest pressures that young children and youth face in their everyday lives. Do not take for granted that they may know these things. Remind them of right and wrong as Luqman reminds his son not to take partners with Allah (swt), the absolute foundation of our faith.

We also understand from this dialogue that we must teach our children what makes a righteous believer, and then give them the tools to implement these characteristics. One such tool is the awareness of Allah (swt) that Luqman puts in his son's mind. It is the knowledge that while a parent is not always watching, Allah (swt) is ever watchful and knows every action that each person engages in— even in what seems like complete isolation. The conclusion of the surah reminds us of this when Allah (swt) explains the infiniteness of His knowledge of generations before us, of the coming of the rain, and of the secrets of the womb.

The youth must also understand from this dialogue the openness of Luqman's son to the wisdom of his father. Allah (swt) has placed each and every one of us in different situations in our lives. So while we will live different lives and face different challenges than our parents, we must never be arrogant and think that they do not know. This surah reminds us to be kind and caring to our parents. It reminds us of the efforts they put forth in raising us. In old age, the needs and interests of the parents should never be ignored. We should honor our parents and always extend the love and kindness they showed us as children.

The story of Luqman also serves as a beautiful reminder to all of us that Luqman was not a prophet of Allah (swt), yet he exemplified the behaviors so pleasing to Allah (swt) that he was made an example for every believer who reflects upon his story. This shows us that every Muslim who strives for it has the ability to attain great pleasure in the eyes of Allah (swt).

Exercises for Surah Luqman

---

1. Address the children in your lives with gentleness.
    a. Try using words similar to Luqman's and address them with "Ya Bunay". You will be reminded of the gentleness of the child and of the wisdom of Luqman.
    b. Use positive reinforcement with your children and make sure you take the time to praise them for the good they do.
2. Young people: listen to the advice of your elders, especially your parents. If you do not agree with them, talk to them and try to understand their perspective, but do not get angry with them. Remember that even if they do not realize that you choose them before other people or things, Allah (swt) is rewarding you.
3. Show special attention to your parents in Ramadan. Increase your closeness to them and your *dua* for them.

Surah As Sajdah (32)

Surah As Sajdah begins with a statement that the Qur'an is a book written by the Lord of the Worlds. How often do we find ourselves fascinated by the writings of scholars? We get excited at the knowledge they have and what they may be able to teach. Allah (swt) is telling us this is the book about life about which He is the expert. Shouldn't we desire to learn from the One who knows better than anyone about our life of tests?

Verse 11[58] reminds us of the time limit that we have on this earth to do good. Allah says that the angels of death will call each of us back to Him.

58

Verse 15 is the verse from which the name of the surah is taken.[59] Allah (swt) is telling us that there are those who have true faith in Allah (swt), in His signs and believe in His Might and Power. It is those servants of Allah (swt) that—when they hear the signs of Allah (swt) recited—they fall down in prostration, or "*sajdah.*" He goes on to describe them as His servants who wake up at night, when no one else is watching, to pray to Him. These are the extra acts of worship that those in these verses are described as performing. What is the position then, in the eyes of Allah, for those of us who are lazy, not only for extra worship, but even for the obligatory worship? What of those who are not mindful of the set times? Or of those who are not mindful of the prayers at all?

Allah (swt) continues to discuss the destination of those who transgress His bounds. The chastisement of such people is severe. During this month, we must reflect on these signs and judge ourselves against them. Are we where we would like to be? Allah (swt) is telling us that if we were to take the time and truly reflect, the understanding of these signs would lead us to fall in prostration.

Verse 24 talks about the criterion for leadership.[60] The leader is patient in adhering to the commands of Allah (swt) and leaving aside what He has prohibited. If the leader adheres to these, then he or she will become a leader who is able to guide people to what is right. We must be cautious about the test of leadership as we see in the story of Musa's people. They began changing and twisting the words of Allah (swt). As a result, they lost their position. From this we see that we must model the behavior in leadership that we would like those following us to

---

[59]Only those believe in Our Signs, who, when they are recited to them, fall down in adoration, and celebrate the praises of their Lord, nor are they (ever) puffed upwith pride.
[60]And We appointed, from among them, leaders, giving guidance under Our command, so long as they persevered with patience and continued to have faith in Our Signs.

exhibit. This is true on all levels, whether in leadership of the home or the community.

Exercises for Surah As Sajdah

---

1. Train your body to work around prayers.
   a. Before sleeping, remind yourself that you want to wake up for *Fajr*.
   b. Reduce activities in the evening that will cause you to compromise your morning prayers.
   c. During the long summer days, reduce your after *Isha* activities and try to sleep after *Isha*.
   d. Be aware of your body's need for sleep and adjust accordingly. If you know you need seven hours of sleep, then make sure you sleep seven hours before *Fajr* time. Remember the goal is to always put Allah (swt) first.
2. Internalize verse 11 before you sleep. And make this *dua* before sleeping: "In Your name my Lord, I lay down and in Your name I rise, so if You should take my soul then have mercy on it. And if you should return it (soul), then protect it in a manner You do so with Your righteous servants." Or recite this dua remembering what a gift sleep can be: "O Allah in Your name I put this body on this bed and in Your name and power, I will rise in the morning"
3. If you are the leader of your house, community, or any other group, write down the things you want to see in those who you lead. Then evaluate if you model those behaviors yourself. If you want your children to be kind to their mother or father, make sure you are kind to your mother or father. If you want the members of your masjid to honor women, then honor them first yourself.

Surah Al Ahzab (33)

The story of Surah Al Ahzab was revealed at a time when the Confederates attempted to surround the Muslim community in Medina in an endeavor to destroy them. The Muslims built a trench around the city to protect themselves from the approaching enemies. Allah (swt) backed their efforts by sending a strong wind that blew away the tents of the enemies, leaving them with no protection from the cold and no ability to start a fire, forcing them to withdraw.

The surah then continues to discuss the resilience of the Muslim community at the time of the Prophet (peace be upon him). We, as a Muslim community in America, feel like there are so many challenges and odds against us. But we can overcome them by steadfastness through solidarity and bonds of brotherhood and sisterhood. But as we do that, we must not forget our own internal community issues.

Surah Al Ahzab speaks about the establishment of the ground rules of social interaction and social behaviors in the Muslim community. It addresses the communal life of Muslims, the social interaction, customs, and habits, as well as their private lives. Specifically, it addresses the social customs and habits that contradict the principles of Islam. It addresses how Islam corrected these behaviors in individuals and in the community and how this is a lesson for us still today. We are reminded that in our private lives and in our interactions with society, we should take only one person as our primary example and model: our beloved Prophet Muhammad (peace be upon him). We should try to live our lives following in his footsteps as Allah (swt) has told us he is the best to follow. We do not have any such example in the world today. In the remaining days of Ramadan, we should try to imagine how we would change our ways or follow his example if he (peace be upon him) was amongst us today.

The surah discusses the behavior of community members with one another and reminds us to adhere to the principles of Islam in our personal and private lives. We have to remember that the revelation has been completed in the life of the Prophet (peace be upon him),and he has set a model for all of humanity—but especially for the Muslim *Ummah*. This was so that we do not just hear his stories but internalize his actions, sayings, and examples, and implement them into our daily lives. We should study his life and learn from the Seerah.

This surah talks about the manner in which to address the Prophet (peace be upon him). It also talks about Muslim women, commanding the believing women to guard their modesty. Today, women are often used as objects. Many people, when trying to sell goods, use women as symbols in their advertisements. In the Qur'an Allah (swt), established protection of a woman's dignity, and her inherent value, over 1400 years ago. She is free from the judgment of others on her physical beauty and is valued based on the beauty of her heart and on the strength of her intellect.

The peak of the surah comes in verse 21, where Allah (swt) establishes a very important principle in terms of our relationship with the Prophet of Allah (peace be upon him).[61] He explains that the success of the Muslims came from the mindset of the believers. They were God-fearing men, led by God-fearing men, including the Prophet Muhammad (peace be upon him). As a result, Allah (swt) rewarded them with victory. We are also given a powerful reminder in verse 36 of the importance of implementing and practicing the commands mentioned above: "It is not befitting for a believer, man or woman, when a matter has been decided by Allah and His Messenger, to have any option about their decision: if anyone disobeys Allah and His Messenger, he is indeed on a clearly wrong path."

---

[61] Ye have indeed in the Messenger of Allah a beautiful pattern (of conduct) for any one whose hope is in Allah and the Final Day, and who engages much in the Praise of Allah.

131

Allah (swt) and His Messenger (peace be upon him) have determined and taught acts of right and wrong and what is acceptable and forbidden. It is not for us to determine what we will practice; rather, it is our responsibility to implement what has been decreed to the best of our ability. Surah Al Ahzab ends with the concept of solidarity within the Muslim community.

Exercises for Surah Al Ahzab

1. If you are under siege or find yourself helpless, remember that Allah (swt) is the one who can change even the most difficult of situations as he did by sending the wind against the enemies of the Prophet (peace be upon him).
2. Sending praise on our Beloved Prophet Muhammad (peace be upon him) will increase love for him in our hearts. Make it a habit to send prayers of peace on him at least ten times a day and do it before you sleep.
3. Take the Prophet as an example in your everyday life. Read a book on the characteristics of the Prophet(peace be upon him) and implement those characteristics into your life one by one.
4. Look at who the role models are in your life (and in the lives of your children). Where does the Prophet of Allah fall in this list? Do the others on the list also hold him (peace be upon him) as their example?

Surah Saba' (34)

Surah Saba' is a Makkan surah that begins with a beautiful verse of praise of Allah (swt), the One to Whom belongs all praise in this life and the next. Verses throughout the Qur'an remind us how those blessed with Paradise enter it with sayings of praise to Allah (swt). Verses 1-29 emphasize the importance of the belief in Allah and the recognition of the truth of His messenger, as well as the importance of defending His name. This surah is named after the civilization of Saba', in the area of Yemen. It was an admired civilization known for its great beauty and comfort. It was full of lush gardens and encompassed every type of natural beauty. Allah (swt) sent messengers to the people of Saba' to encourage them to enjoy the blessings of Allah (swt) and to remain grateful while engaging in that enjoyment. They were reminded that if they were ungrateful, Allah (swt) would not hesitate to replace their life of ease with one of hardship.

The people of Saba' rejected the warnings of the Prophets and did in fact become ungrateful; they turned their backs on the gifts that Allah (swt) had granted them. As a sign, Allah (swt) then sent them the massive flood of 'Aarim. The flood destroyed the dams that protected the city and washed away the gardens they took for granted. He replaced them with gardens that produced bitter fruits. We should understand from this that Allah (swt) is capable of taking back every gift He has given us, as individuals or communities. Therefore, ingratitude is dangerous and is destructive to ourselves. As we have mentioned earlier, Allah (swt) tests the believer both by taking things away *and* by giving things. The people of Saba' are an example of people of great *ni'ma*, blessing, from Allah (swt). They failed their test by being ungrateful. The key to holding on to the favors that Allah (swt) has bestowed upon us is recognizing their place in our lives and thanking Allah (swt) for them.

Surah Saba' also reminds us of the value of what is in the hearts of the servant of Allah (swt). He is not looking at the amount of money we have, the size of our homes, or our physical appearance; rather He is looking for the amount of faith we have in our hearts. Why do we not focus more on our *Iman* and less on the temporary things of this world? In the last verse of this surah Allah reminds us that death ends the pleasure of this life. It removes us from all that we have on this earth, whether we want it to or not. The only service those worldly things will provide us is the manner in which we use them while they are in our possession. Did we use them for the sake of our families? Did we use them to share with others? Or were they merely there to show off?

Zuhd is to detach oneself from the material things of this world. Imam Ali (may Allah be pleased with him) said: "*Zuhd* is for a person to own things but not to let the thing own you."

Exercises for Surah Saba'

1. Allah (swt) does not only test people through loss, as we have seen in the story of Saba'. Look at the blessings in your life. Do not take them for granted or forget what He (swt) has provided for you out of His love and His mercy. These things are also your test. The people of Saba' were not grateful and lost those blessings; how do you compare to their story?

2. Reflect on how attached you are to the material things in your life. If they were gone how would you feel? Think about how much importance these things have in your life. If you find that things are starting to own you instead of you owning things, "fast" from shopping for a week or a month and do something that is beneficial for another person with the money you save.

3. Stop yourself from ever judging people by the clothes they wear or the car they drive.

Surah Fatir (35)

Surah Fatir is a Makkan surah that was revealed before the Hijrah of the Prophet. This surah begins by talking about Allah (swt) as the Creator of the universe, the angels and humans. Allah reminds us of His power in mentioning the rotation of the day and night and the creation of the humans in stages.

In the second verse, Allah (swt) says, "What Allah out of His Mercy doth bestow on mankind, there is none that can withhold: What He doth withhold, there is none that can grant apart from Him." This verse is a firm reminder that Allah's power and plan will succeed and there is nothing that can stop it or force it to happen differently. This shows us that humans do not have power over one another, as is said in the *hadith*, "If all of humanity were to gather together to harm you, they would not be able to do it. And if all of humanity gathered to benefit you, they would not be able to do it."

In verse 10, Allah (swt) talks about *'Izza*, dignity and honor. Allah is the one who grants us everything we have. Why then do we seek approval of people rather Allah (swt)? Allah (swt) is telling us in this verse that color and prestige are not what makes a person accomplished in the eyes of Allah (swt). It is not that which differentiates good people from bad. It is our deeds that determine our true status. The more each of us seeks dignity and honor from Allah, Allah (swt) will elevate them in His eyes among other believers on the Day of Judgment.

In verse 11, Allah reminds us that we were nothing more than dust, and He created us into people and spread us all over the world.[62] If we seek dignity and honor other than from Allah (swt), we should ask ourselves whether or not they are those that possess the power to create us and spread us around the world. If they are not, then for what reason do we need their approval?

In order to understand one's self, we have to understand the history of mankind. The Qur'an wants us to reflect on the lives of those before us. They were civilizations of power, but when Allah exerted His power, there were none that could stop His plan and none that could hide from His strength.

---

[62]And Allah did create you from dust; then from a sperm-drop; then He made you in pairs. And no female conceives, or lays down (her load), but with His knowledge. Nor is a man long-lived granted length of days, nor is a part cut off from his life, but is in a Decree (ordained). All this is easy to Allah.

Exercises for Surah Fatir

---

1. Research the role of angels in Islam. Connect the angels to your personal life by being aware of their presence.
2. Reflect on the meaning of *'Izza*. Think about the ways that you do, or that you should, represent dignity and honor in various aspects of your life.

Surah Ya-Sin (36)

Surah Ya-Sin is the 36th surah of the Qur'an. It was revealed in the Makkan period. Some scholars say that the title of this surah is just two letters with an unknown meaning as occurs in other surahs of the Qur'an. Other say it means, "O Man," calling attention to humanity. Other scholars believe Ya-Sin to be a name of our beloved Prophet Muhammad (peace be upon him), as the third verse says, "You are indeed one of the messengers."

While there is difference of opinion in regard to the meaning of the title, Surah Ya-Sin is known as the Heart of the Qur'an. "Everything has a heart and the heart of the Qur'an is Surah Ya-Sin," (Narrated by Tirmidhi). Surah Ya-Sin is known to be one of the most beautiful surahs of the Qur'an. It also has a powerful effect on the heart of the believer. Surah Ya-Sin provides comfort to people and is recited more frequently in times of difficulty. For the believers who recite it seeking the pleasure of Allah (swt) and the life to come, Allah (swt) will forgive all their previous sins.

Surah Ya-Sin discusses the consequences of refusing the message of Prophet Muhammad (peace be upon him). Specifically, it tells a story of a town that rejected Islam. A man from that town had great blessings of knowledge, but was killed by his people. Allah tells us of the dialogue this person is having in the life to come. This is a reminder forus to stay focused and remember that there is a life after this, the Real Life. We should not allow ourselves to be deceived by the ashes and the dirt of the grave. Allah may make that grave a piece of Paradise for the one buried in it.

Verses 37-40 talk about the vast universe in which we are just tiny specks. Allah (swt) reminds us of the perfect rotation of the sun and the moon, never overlapping. This is one of the miracles of Qur'an: in all of its verses, it never contradicts the science of the world. Then the Qur'an talks about the *Akhirah* and the Day of Judgment. He reminds us that, at the end of it all, we will be brought before Him and will be judged according to what we have done in this life.

This surah concludes with a reminder of the Resurrection. It ends with thestory of a man, Obay ibn Khalaf, who came to the Prophet (peace be upon him) and challenged him. He threw a dry bone to him and asked, "Would your Lord, Allah, be able to resurrect this bone back to life?" Allah (swt) responded by bringing us back to the beginning of our creation and reminding us that He will call us back to Him. We have seen similar connections made in other surahs. Allah (swt) is reminding us that if He brought us to life once out of nothing, He can bring us to life again after death.

Exercises for Surah Ya-Sin

1. Start your day with Surah Ya-Sin.
2. Go outside on a clear night when you can see the stars. Try to identify the different stars and learn what is unique about them.
3. If you are in a difficult situation remember that Allah (swt) says if He wills something to happen all He has to do is say "Be!" and it is. If He has not done something for which you have made *dua*, then remind yourself there is wisdom in it because had He wanted, all He would have had to do is say "Be!"

4. When you are disheartened by the words of others against your religion, read verse 76 as a reminder that Allah (swt) knows what was said and He knows what you feel when no one else does.
5. Read verse 33-40, reflect on the beauty of these signs of Allah (swt). Reflect on who else could so perfectly keep the balance of these signs.

Surah As Saffat (37)

Surah As Saffat is a Makkan surah. It takes its name from the first verse in which we are reminded of the ranks of the angels. The mentioning of them is a reminder to us of the importance of the Angels in the lives of believers. As Muslims it is required for us to believe in the *Mala'ika* of Allah, from the archangel *Jibreel* to the angels that record our every action.

The angels of Allah are constantly in submission to Him. They do not possess the whims and desires that human beings do. As such, persons who control their whims and desires can gain a higher rank, in the eyes of Allah (swt), than even the angels.

Surah As Saffat describes the coming of *Yawm Al Hisab*, the Day of Accountability. Allah (swt) tells us of the sustenance that will be provided to people of Hell Fire and to people of *Jannah*. Surah As Saffat is unique in its description of the Afterlife, as it also talks about the social aspect of the people of *Jannah*. Verses 44-47 give us a description of the peaceful and happy state of the inhabitants of Paradise. He (swt) describes them as sitting on couches facing each other in felicity with nothing around to disturb their cheerful state. It is a place in which people will be joyously reunited with their family and friends of this life. They will be provided food and drink superiorin taste thanany food or drink of this world.

In verses 50-58, we read about the story of a man of

Jannah. He recalls an acquaintance of the *Dunya* and remembers the rejection of the Day of Judgment by the acquaintance. The man of *Jannah* asks Allah if he may see the situation of this other man. Allah (swt) shows him the status of the man in the middle of Hell. The man of *Jannah* then converses with the man of Hell and expresses his victory over their worldly debates. This is evidence that those that will be blessed with Paradise will enjoy everything it offers but will remember their efforts of the *Dunya* and what it took to get there.

Another powerful story in Surah As Saffat is that of Ibrahim (may Allah be pleased with him) and his son Ismael. In a dream, Allah (swt) told Prophet Ibrahim (peace be upon him) to sacrifice his son. Prophet Ibrahim (peace be upon him) responded by informing the young Ismael of his dream. Prophet Ibrahim (peace be upon him) could have concealed the private dream. But he feared Allah (swt), and trusted that he had raised his son to have the same level of *Taqwa*, and therefore, decided to approach his son regarding the dream.

Ismael (may Allah be pleased with him) did not hesitate when he heard the news. In fact, he responded in a comforting manner to his father, encouraging him to fulfill the command of Allah (swt) and reassuring his father of his readiness to obey Allah (swt). Ibrahim and Ismael (peace be upon them both) had proven their commitment to Allah (swt), as their test was greater than any that we are presented with. What could be more difficult than a father sacrificing his child? What would be more difficult than a child being asked to allow his father to sacrifice him? Their test was so significant, yet they did not hesitate for a moment. Would we react the same way?

Allah (swt) will not test our love for Him with the same degree of a test, but He tests us every day. We must reflect on our response when prayer time comes and we have to choose between *salah* and our favorite show or game. Do we rush to

139

Allah's call when the *Adhan* is made, or do we rush to turn the volume up so we don't miss what is said? Do we choose money and business over His command to attend *Jummah* prayer? Do we choose excessive luxury over fulfilling the command to give due portion of our wealth to the poor? The tests presented to us are infinitely smaller than what was presented to Prophet Ibrahim (peace be upon him) and his son, but the question remains the same: where does Allah (swt) fall on our list of priorities?

Exercises for Surah As Saffat

1. Learn the names and responsibilities of the *Mala'ika of Allah*.
2. Imagine yourself in the description of Paradise. What things do you need to start doing or stop doing to get there? Remember it is never too late to start on a path towards Paradise.
3. Prophet Ibrahim(peace be upon him) was asked to sacrifice the thing most beloved to him, his own son. While we will never be asked to do the same, what things would you sacrifce in your life if Allah (swt) commanded? Think about how easily you would give it up. If there is something that you would struggle to separate from, write it down and find ways to detach it from your heart. It is okay to keep it, but do not let it own you.
4. Each day, if you have delayed your prayer, look at what stopped you and write those things down. Spend the next few days, weeks, or months, to overcome those distractions until your prayers are the first thing you do when prayer time comes.

Surah Saad (38)

This Makkan surah takes its name from the lone letter that isthe first verse of the surah. It is believed that the beginning verses of this surah were revealed in response to the *Quraysh* trying to dissuade Abu Talib from supporting his nephew, the Prophet Muhammad (peace be upon him). They asked him to tell the Prophet (peace be upon him) to stop talking about Islam. The Prophet (peace be upon him) told his uncle he only wanted this one sentence from them. Abu Jahal, the Prophet's other uncle, said he would give him that sentence and 10 more like it. The Prophet asked for the following sentence: "There is no god except God and Muhammad is the Messenger of God." They responded with verse 5: "Has he made gods (all) into one God?" They questioned as to why Allah (swt) had sent Prophet Muhammad (peace be upon him) and not someone else. Allah responds to their arrogance in verses 9 and 10, by asking if they know better than Him about the universe and what it consists of. It is in these 10 verses that Allah (swt) reminds us of the ruin that came to generations before them because they rejected the Messengers of Allah (swt), as the *Quraysh* rejected Prophet Muhammad (peace be upon him).

Surah Saad talks about Dawud (may Allah be pleased with him) and the exceptional amount of strength and patience he had. Despite how he was mocked by his enemies, he depended on Allah (swt). Allah (swt) tells us that Dawud's patience led him to win and, as a result, Allah (swt) granted him kingship. Sulayman, the son of Dawud (may Allah be pleased with them both), was granted both Prophethood and kingship by Allah (swt). Sulayman (peace be upon him) was tested with wealth and calamity. He had the unique gift from Allah (swt) that jinn and wind were subservient to him. As kings, they were granted numerous blessings and gifts. Allah (swt) is reminding us in this surah that, even for men with all of these blessings, seeking forgiveness is necessary for all humans. We have reviewed many stories of the Prophets of Allah asking forgiveness from their Lord. How many times a day do we seek Allah's forgiveness? Are we less in need of it than His own Messengers?

This surah also talks about the story of Prophet Ayyub (peace be upon him) and the use of patience. Allah (swt) reminds us that people exert patience in good times and in bad. Allah (swt) encourages patience but not patience that leads us to things outside the boundaries of Islam. There are some who—when Allah (swt) tests them—are not able to be patient and to understand there is a purpose and reason for their test. But when *Shaytan* presents them with temptation, they exercise great amounts of patience in following their desires. This stubborn type of patience will only further lead to the path of *Shaytan*. We should reflect on where we use our patience. Are we being patient when our parents or children ask for our time or energy? Are we patient in illness and calamity like our Prophet Ayyub (may Allah be pleased with him)? Or are we patient in staying up through the night to watch movies with themes and images contradictory to our faith? Are we patient in listening to gossip about our brothers and sisters at the *Masjid*? Allah (swt) calls us to be patient; we must make that patience something that brings us closer to Him. Allah (swt) reminds us in verses 41-43 that patience in His way comes with reward in this life and the next.

May Allah (swt) make us among those who are patient in His way.

Exercises for Surah Saad

1. Evaluate your level of patience in various aspects of your life. Remember the patience of Dawud (May Allah be pleased with him).
   a. Take your time in your prayer without rushing. See how patient you are particularly after standing for an extended period of time in *Taraweeh*.
   b. Monitor how much patience you have with your children and think of ways that you can increase your level of patience.

  c. Compare your patience with things pleasing to Allah (swt) with those that are not pleasing to Allah (swt). Are you more patient spending time watching TV shows and long sports events then you are with your family or your prayers?

2. Establish a spiritual support system. First establish this within your family. Then surround yourself with friends, family and others, who have morals and values similar to your own principles in practicing Islam. If you have children, start the circle for them early. Surround them with both adults who practice the same values and children who are also being raised with the same principles.

3. Verses 25-27 explain the racism of *Iblis*. Make it a commitment to never allow yourself to follow his example of racism or any other matter by protecting the rights of all people regardless of their ethnicity or language.

Surah Az Zumar(39)

Surah Az Zumar is a Makkan surah. The topic of this surah is the Qur'an itself. Allah (swt) tells us that the Qur'an is a source of guidance from Him. He reminds us that the Qur'an speaks to every person. Those who abandon the message of the Qur'an do so because of their lack of desire to receive its message. This surah talks about the hardness of their hearts and that the Qur'an can enter their hearts if they are willing to receive it. Unfortunately, today we see many people living life in fear of another person's judgment. Allah (swt) reminds us that if we commit ourselves to our faith, He is capable of making us feel the sense of comfort many people are often searching for.

  Some say it is easier to go out in a non-Muslim environment and dress as society dictates. But Allah (swt) is telling us if we sincerely make an effort to complete the commands He has placed on us, He will provide the promised ease that many of us long for. This is greater than any blessing a person can ask for in a material world. Allah (swt) has made Islam easy for us. It is not a task or a hardship. By committing to practice our religion in all of its aspects throughout the year, not only in this Blessed month, we will gain the sense of pride in our Muslim identity that we see in those who fought to establish our *Deen*.

In verses 29 and 30, Allah (swt) is calling us to reflect on who has final authority over our decisions. Allah (swt) commands us to enjoin what He has decreed as good and leave that which He has forbidden. And for those who follow this, there is the greatest reward of all rewards: Paradise. We have also reviewed in previous surahs that Allah (swt) has commanded for us what is good for us, though we may not know it, and has forbidden what is bad for us. Therefore, if we live our lives making decisions based on this book of guidance that Allah (swt) has blessed us with out of His infinite wisdom and mercy, we will live meaningful and happy lives, with an even greater destination in the next life. We must reflect, though, whether this is truly our measurement for making our decisions. How often do we choose one action or another based on the acceptance we may get from other creations (our peers) instead of the Creator Himself?

Allah (swt) ends this surah with a beautiful description of the masses of people walking to *Jannah* and the scene of being greeted at Paradise's doors by the angels with a greeting of peace and people joining them in praising Allah (swt) as an acknowledgement of His fulfilled promise.

Surah Az Zumar also contains a beautiful verse 53 in which Allah (swt) reminds His creation that there is no situation in which people will find themselves where they cannot return to Allah (swt) seeking His forgiveness. Allah (swt) reminds us that despite all that we may have done to wrong our own souls, He is always willing to forgive. We must remember this in this

Blessed month when Allah (swt) has opened His doors of mercy and forgiveness.

May Allah (swt) grant us forgiveness this Ramadan and make us a community of Paradise.

Exercises for Surah Az Zumar

1. Understand the process of repentance.
   a. Acknowledge the actions that require repentance because denying them will not help you move toward correcting the actions.
   b. Stop the action immediately. When the sin has reached the point of addiction, correcting it will take time. Make the resolution to start the recovery process immediately.
   c. Have strong determination to overcome that problem.
   d. Stop dwelling on the past but acknowledge that something that required change did happen.
   e. Choose friends and people who can support you in your process of repentance and will encourage you to do what is right.
   f. Never despair of the mercy of Allah (swt). Never lose hope. Identify major sins and make a plan forhow to get rid of them. Remember that on Hajj stones are gathered at one location and thrown at a representation of Shaytan. Seeking forgiveness is a process.
2. Make *istighfar*, seek forgiveness, throughout the day. This can be while you wait, ride the bus, a few minutes before or after prayer, or on a walk.

Surah Ghafir (40)

Surah Ghafir (Forgiver) is the 40th surah in the Holy Qur'an and

145

is also known as "Mu'min" (Believer). Surah Ghafir begins the set of seven surahs starting with "Ha Meem." It was revealed in the Makkan period around the same time as the other six surahs of its set. The title of the surah is taken from the third verse in which Allah (swt) refers to His attribute of "the One who Forgives."

Allah mentions forgiveness many times throughout the surah, reminding the reader that regardless of the past deeds in a person's life, Allah (swt) is always ready to forgive His servant. We have heard many descriptions of the consequences faced by civilizations that rejected the truth of Allah (swt). But Allah (swt) reminds us that while His wrath is strong, His mercy is greater: "My Mercy is before My wrath."

In verse 66, Allah (swt) reaffirms the order for *Tawhid* and tells Prophet Muhammad (peace be upon him) to inform the idol worshipers about the prohibition to worship anything other than Allah (swt). But they offered Prophet Muhammad (peace be upon him) many things that they thought he wanted, in the hope of him giving up the call to Islam. He (peace be upon him)refused all they offered, as he knew none of those things would gain Allah's pleasure. We see from this example how Allah (swt) was the Prophet's final reference point in all matters. The commands of Allah (swt) were his measure for right and wrong and he did not allow anything to alter that standard. Our beloved Prophet (peace be upon him)was engaging the most powerful tribe of Arabia regarding their most cherished worshipping rituals. Though the environment was hostile, he remained true to his commitment to Allah (swt). Do we give the commands of Allah (swt) the priority in guiding our decisions? Or do we let people and things around us determine how we will handle situations that Allah (swt) is testing us with?

In verse 68, Allah (swt) says that He is the One who holds the key to creating life and causing life to cease existence.[63] He is the One capable of conducting anything on earth and all He needs to do in order for that to happen is say, "Be," and it happens. As such, there is nothing in this world or the next that can be attained without Him. Why, then, do we carelessly disregard the commands of Allah (swt) in order to obtain money or status or prestige, when He is the source of everything and byone word He can grant it to us? Therefore, we must obtain what we want through obeying His command and asking for His help.

Surah Ghafir brings our attention to our work in this world. It calls us to be mindful of our deeds now rather than when death comes upon us, and we cannot change what is on our scale. We are reminded through various verses in this surah of the regret that people will feel when they see the punishment of the Fire. They will wish they had lived their lives differently and will ask why they were not warned, or if they can be forgiven and have their punishment lightened. The warnings of the Messenger of Allah (swt) came and the opportunity to seek forgiveness was present every day. Did we take advantage of these opportunities? Allah (swt) is telling us this in order to remind us that the time for us to change is not tomorrow, or next month, or next Ramadan. The time to improve ourselves and bring ourselves closer to Allah (swt) is right now. As Allah (swt) reminded us at the beginning of the surah and by its title, He is the most Merciful and most Forgiving. Allah has blessed us again with these beautiful last 10 days of Ramadan; let us make the most of them by committing to leave behind the habits that we have been able to abstain from and commit to maintaining the spiritual connection with Allah that we have built during this time.

May Allah (swt) forgive all our sins and make us amongst the people of Paradise.

---

[63] It is He Who gives Life and Death; and when He decides upon an affair, He says to it, "Be", and it is.

Exercises for Surah Ghafir

1. Remind yourself of the importance of connecting to Allah (swt). Read the translation and *tafsir* of verse 60.
2. Practice the best ways of making *dua*.
   a. Always maintain unshakable belief that Allah (swt) listens to and responds to every supplication. Do not let your relationship with Allah (swt) be only when you are struck with calamity. If you do not see the response to your supplication, remember that the response in not promised on your calendar but on Allah's. Remember there are some supplications for which the response is saved for paradise.
   b. When you supplicate to Allah (swt), begin your supplication with praise of Allah (swt).
   c. Follow the example of Zakariya and declare your weaknesses.
   d. Look for the best times to make *dua* and repeat it often. Some of the best times are during the last third of the night, during the prostration in your prayer, during rain, between the *adhan* and the *iqamah*, when sick, or during times of traveling. At the Mount of Arafat and standing at the door of the Ka'bah are amongst the best places to make *dua*.
   e. Conclude your *dua* with praise of the Beloved Prophet of Allah (peace be upon him).
3. The supplication of one person on behalf of another in their absence is a powerful supplication. This Ramadan chose a supplication partner and make *dua* for each other on a daily basis.

7

Surah Fussilat to Surah Al Nas

Surah Fussilat (41)

Surah Fussilat is the second of the group of seven surahs beginning with "Ha Meem." It is also known by the name "Ha Meem." Surah Fussilat is the 41st surah of the Qur'an. This surah discusses how the foundation of faith and revelation is Allah's Power, Mercy and Forgiveness. It also deals with Resurrection and the Day of Judgment and the evidence of its existence.

In verses 10 and 11, Allah (swt) gives a powerful example of His authority. He mentions the mountains He has created on earth, a source of water supplying regions of the world, and bringing forth life and sustenance. Allah (swt) also talks about the fusion of the sky and the earth. He tells the two to come together and they respond "in willing obedience." The verses that follow continue explaining how He then divided the heavens into seven levels and charged each with its specific duty. How does one question the capabilities of Allah (swt) when we see that even the sky and the earth acknowledge His infinite power and obey without question? Everything in the universe praises His name and submits to His will.

In verse 22 through 25, Allah (swt) provides us with a scene, in contrast to that in *Zumar*, of the people entering Hell. In these verses, He describes the terrifying scene of the masses moving towards the Fire. Those who rejected the signs of Allah (swt) will be brought before the Fire and the body will tell the truth of the deeds committed. The person will ask why their own body is speaking against them: "They will say to their skins:

'Why bear ye witness against us?' They will say: '(Allah) hath given us speech—(He) Who giveth speech to everything: He created you for the first time, and unto Him were ye to return,'" (41:21). What will our eyes, our ears, our hands, and our tongues tell Allah (swt) on that Day?

In verse 25, Allah (swt) speaks of the companions of the people of Hellfire: "And We have destined for them intimate companions of like nature, who made alluring to them what was before them and behind them." This is in reference to those whom they took as friends or leaders in this life. Allah (swt) is reminding us that they, too, are creations of Allah (swt) and in the end they, too, will be brought before Him for judgment. We must understand from this verse that we cannot take as close companions those who are not mindful of the path of Allah (swt). They will lead people astray, but they will not carry the consequences of anyone's actions other than their own. We should work to always surround ourselves with people who live each moment of their lives with firm belief in Allah (swt), people who base each decision on what is pleasing to Him. If we keep such company around us, then when Allah (swt) tests us alone, we will have trained our soul to make the decisions that are more pleasing to Him.

In verse 39, Allah (swt) prompts another reminder for those who remain in doubt of the Day of Resurrection. They question the possibility of Allah (swt) bringing back what is dead. Allah (swt) reminds us that He brings back the earth after it is dry and barren. He sends the rain from the heavens and brings the life back to the earth.

In verse 43, Allah (swt) brings back to our attention the Oneness of His message.[64] The words of Allah (swt) have always been, are, and will always be that Allah (swt) is Merciful and

---

[64]Nothing is said to thee that was not said to the apostles before thee: that thy Lord has at His Command (all) forgiveness as well as a most Grievous Penalty.

Forgiving to His servants and is Just in His retribution to those who reject.

---

1. Reflect on who are your closest friends and companions. Will these people lead you towards Allah (swt)? If not, are they leading you away from Him and are you following their lead? Remind yourself whenever you spend time with them that, if they are leading you away from Allah to things that are outside the boundaries of Islam, they may be leading you now, but on the Day of Judgment they will not be of any help to you. You will stand alone and answer for what actions you engaged in. Lineage and company do not secure paradise; good works do.
2. Do you share your religion with your friends? When you are in the company of others, do you represent what Islam is by your example or through discussion? Share Islam with those around you and do so in the best way possible. Remember, you cannot and should not force Islam on any person. Be gentle in your *da'wah*; do it through conduct and integrity.
3. Reach out to someone who has wronged you, particularly any family members. Be kinder to someone who has not been kind to you.

Surah Ash Shura (42)

Surah Ash Shura is the 42nd surah of the Qur'an. It is a Makkan surah named after the important Islamic concept of consultation and seeking counsel when making decisions. *Shura* is one of the most important concepts that we as Muslims should apply in our everyday lives, in our families and in our communities. It humbles us and requires that we admit our shortcomings and limitations.

Allah (swt) has also mentioned the concept of *Shura* in Surah Al Imran. Following the Battle of *Uhud*, the beloved Prophet (peace be upon him) had given his companions a suggestion. The *shura* of the companions was to do other than what he (peace be upon him) had suggested. The Prophet, being a humble leader, went with the *shura*, but consequently lost the battle. Allah (swt) sent the Qur'an to remind Prophet Muhammad (peace be upon him) that, despite the results, it is necessary to continue consulting with the companions.

This is a lesson to us that being right does not mean we should become arrogant and no longer seek *shura*; rather, we should continue to learn from others' perspectives and ideas in order to make sound decisions. As we do this, we must make sure that we create an inviting and encouraging environment for those involved in contributing to the *shura*. We should establish a platform for ideas to be formulated and shared. In terms of leadership, there are a few amongst us who may need to consider how to incorporate consultation within our community. This example, however, is not only relevant to those in leadership but,in fact is relevant among one another.

Through this example, we see that the Prophet (peace be upon him) consulted with those close to him. We must try to do the same within our families, be it spouses, or parents with their children or children with their parents. Parents, when making decisions, you should try to consult with your children. Though it is the parents' responsibility to make decisions that are sound for the overall family, including all the children, it is good to establish the lines of communication that include hearing their feedback, opinions, and perspective on matters that will affect them. Likewise, children and young adults should feel comfortable seeking consultation with their parents and older family members to benefit from the experience they have to offer and to learn from it as well.

Verse 36 directs us to be people who are *Akhirah*-oriented, people who are mindful of their responsibilities, rights, and restrictions in this life, all with the reward of the Afterlife as their primary goal. The *Dunya* is nothing but a passing moment. We can enjoy the time that we have here but as Allah (swt) tells us in verse 37, we must avoid crossing any boundaries while we are here. Verse 38 connects the concept of *iman*, faith, and the establishment of prayers with the concept of shura. It establishes rituals of Zakah as a means for teaching unity and care within communities.

Surah Ash Shura ends beautifully with the remembrance of Allah (swt) and the importance of the Qur'an. It is a reminder that it was revealed for us, and that whatever we do in our personal lives or in the community should be based on what it instructs. The Qur'an is a source of life. It is our anchor point, a light that guides the community to the straight path.

May Allah (swt) strengthen our relationship with the Qur'an in this beautiful month and help us to continue that relationship throughout the year. May He make it the light of our hearts and our guide to Him (swt).

Exercises for Surah Ash Shura

1. Shura is to accept that your opinion might not be the best. In order to be effective, shura has to be based on mutual respect. The next time you seek *shura*, seek it with an open mind.
2. When giving advice, do not be arrogant. Have the person's interests at heart and his or her feelings in mind.
3. When giving advice, do so in private unless the advice is necessary for the public.

Surah Az Zukhruf (43)

The name of this surah comes from the 35th verse in which Allah (swt) reminds us that the luxuries of this life are not given to those who are better than others; rather luxuries are provided as a test.[65] True luxuries are in the life to come, which Allah (swt) has reserved for the righteous amongst us. This verse falls in a group of verses discussing the reality of this life as a temporary life. If persons were to have all the comfort and material pleasures of gold and wealth, but live in disbelief of Allah, then all of their pleasures would be temporary. If they chose to use this gift of the *Dunya* in the way of Allah (swt) and in the way of charitable giving, then they will carry the weight of such righteousness into the life to come. If Allah (swt) favored the wealthy, would He send an orphan as a leader for humanity, the most perfect of mankind? If Allah (swt) favored the wealthy, would the Prophet of Allah have been a man who often went to sleep at night on an empty stomach?

In verses 43 and 44, Allah (swt) reminds us of the many things in this life that question our commitment to Him. Allah (swt) said to His Prophet (peace be upon him), "Hold fast onto what was revealed to you." Allah (swt) is reminding us not to compromise the principles of the Qur'an because if we remain with the Qur'an, we are on the straight path. A community that takes the Qur'an as their guide will flourish and excel, for Allah (swt) has explained that the community who lives by the Qur'an is an honored community.

Allah (swt) tells us the importance of choosing good friends. Close friends are not those who have the greatest prestige or are wealthy; they are the ones who have the best hearts. There is a danger in friendships that may distance you from Allah (swt) or that will take you away from Allah (swt). He reminds us that on the Day of Judgment, friends are enemies of each other except those that are righteous people. As we establish our lives and start our families, it is important for young parents to choose righteous friends to share their time

---

[65]Nothing is said to thee that was not said to the apostles before thee: that thy Lord has at His Command (all) forgiveness as well as a most Grievous Penalty.

with as we are in a way choosing the company and environment that our children will have.

In verse 67, Allah (swt) warns us to be mindful of whom we select as friends. For the youth, this verse is one that you should carry with you each day. Each day that you go to school, you face social and peer pressures that do not always encourage or facilitate actions toward what Allah (swt) has decreed as good. As you choose your friends, know that the only true friends are those that will encourage you to do what is good for you. True friends do not encourage each other to engage in behaviors harmful to their body or their soul. The pressure that society places on people is strong, so we must choose friends that will encourage and support us to accept the things that are decreed as good and to avoid the things that are evil.

Exercises for Surah Az Zukhruf

1. When you wake up each morning, remind yourself that you are on the path of Allah (swt).
2. Read the translation and *tafseer* of verse 17. Look at your relationship with women in your life. Address misconceptions and misunderstandings of treatment of women in Islam. Start by being the example within your own family.
3. Learn the *Dua* of Traveling: "Allah is the greatest, Allah is the greatest, Allah is the greatest, Allah is the greatest, How perfect He is, The One who has placed this transport at our service, and we ourselves would not have been capable of that, and to our Lord is our final destiny. O Allah, we ask You for *birr* and *taqwah* in this journey of ours, and we ask You for deeds which please You. O Allah, facilitate our journey and let us cover its distance quickly. O Allah, You are The Companion on the journey and the Successor over the family, O Allah, I take refuge with You from the

difficulties of travel, from having a change of heart and being in a bad predicament, and I take refuge in You from an ill fated outcome with wealth and family."

Surah Ad Dukhan (44)

Surah Ad Dukhan is a Makkan surah that gets its name from verse 10.[66] Dukhan, "the smoke," is interpreted as smoke that filled the sky during the famine in Makkah. The Quraysh needed the rain and asked Prophet Muhammad (peace be upon him) to supplicate to Allah (swt) for the smoke to be removed and for Him (swt) to send down rain. Their *du'a* was answered, yet they still disbelieved.

One of the most important themes of this surah is *Laylatul Qadr*. *Laylatul Qadr* is said to be a night in the last 10 nights of Ramadan, particularly on an odd night. As we enjoy the last 10 nights of Ramadan, we should seek to collect all the blessings of it that we can. Allah (swt) accepts the *du'a* of every person who calls upon Him (swt) on that night.

Aisha (may Allah be pleased with her) asked the Prophet of Allah what supplication she should make during these nights. The Prophet (peace be upon him) replied with: "O Allah, You are forgiving and most generous. You love to forgive, so forgive me."

The Qur'an was revealed on this blessed night in the month of Ramadan. The people of *Quraysh* were sleeping when the revelation came down. The month of Ramadan is a celebration of that beautiful night. In the last third of each night, Allah (swt) offers to accept the *du'a* of any of His servants. He specifically looks for any of believers seeking forgiveness so that He may forgive them. Just as the *Quraysh* slept through the Night of the Revelation, many Muslims sleep through the many

---

[66]Then watch thou for the Day that the sky will bring forth a kind of smoke (or mist) plainly visible,

opportunities that Allah (swt) offers us to be closer to Him (swt). Sometimes the sleep is literal, such as sleeping through the last third of each night. And sometimes that sleep is figurative, being unconscious of Allah (swt) and of our responsibilities. Do we really take the opportunity to make more *du'a* when it is raining, between the *Adhan* and the *Iqama*, or when we are sick? These are times that Allah (swt) has opened the doors of supplication even wider and is waiting for anyone who takes such opportunities to speak with him.

We must remember that Allah (swt) is never in need of sleep. He is always aware and ready to hear the call of anyone who calls upon Him (swt) at any time of any day throughout the year.

Exercises for Surah Ad Dukhan

1. As you seek *Laylatul Qadr*, focus on making *dua* to Allah (swt), not on looking for the physical signs of the night. Consider every night of the last ten nights to be *Laylatul Qadr*. Do not put everything into one night and then forget the rest of the nights.
2. In Ramadan we practice abstaining from that which is permissible to us. When the days of Ramadan have gone, and we eagerly await next Ramadan, we need to use the training of abstaining to abstain from all things forbidden to us.
3. Learn the *dua* that the Prophet Muhammad (peace be upon him) taught to Aisha (May Allah be pleased with her): "O Allah, You are forgiving and most generous. You love to forgive, so forgive me."

Surah Al Jathiya(45)

Surah Al Jathiya is the 45th surah of the Qur'an. *Jathiya* means "the kneeling down." This is taken from verses 28 and 29, in which Allah (swt) is referring to those people who mocked His signs. They did not take Allah's words and signs seriously and, as a result, they would be brought to their knees before Allah (swt) and their actions of rejection would not benefit them.

Surah Al Jathiya begins with a theme that is common across the "Ha Meem" surahs, verses specifically discussing the Qur'an. This surah connects the signs of Allah (swt) in the universe to the verses of the Qur'an, both of which are referred to as "signs." As Muslims, we need to look at both of these together as that is a confirmation of belief. Some people try to read the signs of the universe without reading the divine revelation, the Qur'an. Others read the Qur'an but do not reflect on the signs of the universe. Allah (swt) is reminding us that in order to truly understand His signs and enjoy the beauty and the benefit they bring, we must connect them and reflect on those connections.

Allah (swt) calls us to see the truth of His signs not only in our minds but also in our hearts. In verse 15, Allah (swt) says whoever recognizes His signs and uses them to live a righteous life, they will do good for themselves. Whoever does good does so for the benefit of his own soul and whoever does harm does so at the expense of his own soul. Not reflecting on spiritual guidance leaves a person in darkness, without criteria of right or wrong. A person who rejects the guidance of the Qur'an is like a student who refuses to study for an exam even after continuously failing. The instructor tells him to read the book but he insists on attempting without it. How can we then expect to understand the ways to navigate through life's tests if we refuse to read the directions? How can we expect to pass the test if we never sought to learn the answers?

The Qur'an is our guide in Ramadan and throughout our lives. It is a gift and a blessing from our Lord, the All Knowing. Let us use it to guide us through the end of this month and throughout the coming year.

Exercises for Surah Al Jathiya

---

1. Connect the signs of Allah (swt) in the world with the signs in His book. Read the signs in the Qur'an and reflect on those signs in the universe.

2. Look at verse 20 and ask yourself if there is anything that you do in the *dunya* at the expense of the *akhirah*. If so, what are other things you can do or have in the *dunya* as substitute for your actions that do not compromise your *akhirah*?

3. Remember that your every action is being written in a book that you will be given on the Day of Judgment. Spend one day writing down every single thing you do, the good things in one column and the mistakes in another. Evaluate your day to see how did you do?

Surah Al Ahqaf(46)

Surah Al Ahqaf is the last of the "Ha Meem" surahs. *Al Ahqaf* is the plural of *"hiqaf,"* carving in the sand. Ahqaf is the name of the place where the people of *'Ad,* who were destroyed by wind, dwelled.. Allah (swt) can humble a person or an entire civilization as a result of their disobedience. Surah Al Ahqaf shows not only the great power of Allah (swt), but also emphasizes the great limitation of human power.

The people of *'Ad* were thought to be the mightiest civilization and Allah (swt) destroyed them with mere wind. They did not heed His signs and were then themselves made an example for others. In verses 32-34, Allah (swt) reminds us that whoever does not respond to the call of Allah (swt), they will not be able to find any supporters against His will. There is no advantage for the person who deviates from Allah's path. He (swt) does not need our obedience to sustain Himself in anyway. Rather, He is inviting us to be obedient so that we may prosper in this life and in the next.

In verses 14-18, Allah (swt) talks about the command forpe ople to show kindness to their parents. Allah (swt) teaches us that those who attain the age of 40 and continue to show kindness to parents through speech, actions, and supplications on their behalf, Allah (swt) has a reward of Paradise for them. He also promises to overlook their sins. Here Allah (swt) is connecting power to kindness. He talks about the struggle of the mother to care for the child and the child returning the kindness and care. Similarly, Allah (swt) talks about the child that is not grateful to his or her parents. Allah (swt) says those people who do not show kindness and mercy to their parents do not deserve the Mercy of Allah (swt).

"O my Lord! Grant me that I may be grateful for Your favor which You have bestowed on me, and upon both my parents, and that I may work righteousness such as you may approve; and be gracious to me in my issue. Truly have I turned to You and truly do I bow to You in submission." [46:16]

Exercises for Surah Al Ahqaf

1. Remember the people of 'Ad and think about how much you strive to have more wealth or higher status. These are not bad things unless you use them in a manner displeasing to Allah (swt). As you establish your home on earth and expand it, remember that wealth and power should not lead to arrogance or being neglectful of the signs of Allah (swt).
2. Learn the following dua from Surah Ahqaf: "O my Lord! Grant me that I may be grateful for Your favor which You have bestowed on me, and upon both my parents, and that I may work righteousness such as You may approve; and be gracious to me in my issue. Truly have I turned to You and truly do I bow to You in Submission." 46:16

Surahs Muhammad, Al Fath, Al Hujurat, An Najm (47, 48, 49, 53)

The first three surahs are Madinan surahs, while Surah An Najm is Makkan. However, they share the common discussion of Allah (swt) asserting the authority of His final Prophet, Muhammad (peace be upon him). There are only a few verses in the Qur'an that mention Prophet Muhammad (peace be upon him) by his name, as Allah (swt) often refers to him as "*Rasul*" and "*Nabi*" in order to establish his authority. He was the only prophet and messenger at that time. These surahs build a deep level of respect and love for our beloved Prophet (peace be upon him).

The grandfather of the Prophet (peace be upon him)gave him the beautiful name Muhammad so he would be praised in this life and the next. He certainly could not have envisioned the level of praise our beloved prophet would receive. The 47th surah of the Holy Qur'an, Surah Muhammad, takes the Prophet's name and honors him in the book of Allah (swt). Allah (swt) also shows praise of him in the first verses of Surah Al Fath. In verse 33 of Surah Muhammad, Allah (swt) tells us to obey Him and after such a weighty command, He tells us to obey His Messenger, Muhammad (peace be upon him).

In Surah Al Fath, the role of the Prophet (peace be upon him) is established as a glad tiding to mankind. Allah (swt) explains the nearness of Prophet Muhammad (peace be upon him) to Him. Allah (swt) is telling us in Surah Al Fath that those who give their allegiance to the Prophet of Allah (peace be upon him) are giving their allegiance to Allah (swt) and when they commit to the Prophet of Allah (peace be upon him), they are committing to Allah (swt). These descriptions show us the level of honor that has been granted to His Final Prophet (peace be upon him). It is also made clear in Surah Al Fath that belief in Muhammad (peace be upon him) as the final messenger of Allah (swt) is a vital part of our faith. We cannot ignore his position in our faith or disregard the examples and lessons he left behind for us.

Surah Hujarat reminds us of the uniqueness of this Prophet (peace be upon him) and that he is not like any other person. Those in his company were taught never to speak in a loud voice. After the Prophet (peace be upon him) passed away, this act of respect was maintained in his mosque and in people's dealings with each other. This was his nature, to never speak in a harsh or loud manner. It is a lesson to us that even when we speak about him, we should remember that he was not just any other person. He was a man loved and honored by Allah Almighty. Is there any greater honor than the honor given by the Creator? Therefore, we should all make it a habit, from this moment, to follow the mention of the name of Prophet Muhammad with "Salalahu 'Alayhi wasalam," prayers and peace be upon him.

In Surah Muhammad, Allah (swt) is asking the believers to give in His way by supporting Prophet Muhammad (peace be upon him). Allah (swt) recognizes that humans are not capable of parting with all of their possessions and wealth, so He only asks for a portion. He reminds us that there are those of us who are stingy, but our stinginess will only hurt our own souls in this life and the next. Ramadan is a time of sacrifice, controlling the desires, and giving of the self. Let us be of those who give in the way of Allah (swt).

In Surah Hujurat, Allah (swt) reminds us of the lesson we have learned from the past few surahs. Allah (swt) reminds us in this surah that we should not make decisions after He and His Messenger have determined something for us. In other words, as we have read before, we must use Allah (swt) and the Prophet Muhammad (peace be upon him) as our standard in determining what course of action we will take in our lives.

Surah Al Hujurat also reminds us that He has made us

into people from all different nations and tribes so that we may know and love one another. This powerful verse is an example of what the *Ummah* of the Prophet (peace be upon him) implemented—something that all of our communities should also work to establish. Allah (swt) did not create us differently to quarrel and dispute over our differences, but to embrace them and love each other for them. Let this be a challenge to all of us in this blessed month of Ramadan to meet someone from a different background than ourselves and get to know that person. Allah (swt) has established the Prophet's example as something for us to follow. Bringing down the walls of differences that stand between us is one of the many examples we should work to emulate. Surah Al Hujurat tells us that following the Prophet's example will lead to harmony; individually and within our communities.

Surah An Najm also talks about the Prophet Muhammad's journey of *Al 'Isra'* and *Mi'raj*. It gives us a description of the purity of our beloved Prophet's speech, sight, and mind. It also talks about his teacher, *Jibreel* (may Allah be pleased with him). The teacher of the Prophet was an angel of Allah (swt), and a regular visitor in the house of the *Rasul*. This surah continues on to remind us to distance ourselves from all sins, but especially to distance ourselves from the great sins. Allah (swt) knows we will fall into error, but He tells us that as long as we avoid the major sins, He will overlook the minor ones. He then goes on to remind us that our final destination lies in our hands. We will be given what we strive toward.

O Allah, make us amongst the people who distance themselves from matters displeasing to You and help us to follow the example of our beloved Prophet Muhammad (peace be upon him)in all aspects of our life.

Exercises for Surah Muhammad, Al Fath, Al Hujurat, An Najm

---

1. Read the *seerah*, life of the Prophet (peace be upon him).
2. Do activities with your children around the Prophet (peace be upon him), his life and his characteristics.
3. Make ten *salawat* on the Prophet(peace be upon him) each night before you sleep.
4. Make the poetry and songs about the Prophet (peace be upon him) a replacement for other entertainment.
5. As you read the *seerah*, write down the actions and characteristics you read about. Take one at a time and incorporate those things into your own life.
6. Read a book on *hadith* to understand its place in a Muslim's life. In regards to this, Allah (swt) says "O Ye who believe! Put not yourselves forward before Allah and His Messenger, but fear Allah. For Allah is He Who hears and knows all things." 49:1

Surahs Qaf, Adh Dhariyat, At Tur, Al Qamar (50, 51, 52, 54)

These four Makkan surahs share a common theme of confirming the authority of the Qur'an. Both the Qur'an and the final Prophet (peace be upon him) are described as bearers of glad tidings and as warners to mankind. In Surah Qaf, Allah (swt) connects His signs of the universe with those of the Qur'an. He uses the signs of the sky, the mountains and the rain. In Surah Adh Dhariyat Allah (swt) uses the wind to call the reader's attention to His knowledge of His creation. These beautiful verses not only establish the Qur'an as an authority but they establish a love for the Qur'an in our hearts.

In all of these surahs lah (swt) mentions surahthe previous generations. They were generations who had various types of strength, power, and wealth, but they did not acknowledge Allah (swt) and they were not grateful to Him. As a result they all faced different consequences that ended in their destruction, including the people of Lut, Nuh, Fir'awn, Ad, and Thamud. Their stories are all a part of these surah sand are warnings for us to take notice of the signs of Allah (swt) before He removes our opportunity to do so. Surah Al Qamar follows the mentionof misguided generations before us with an emphasis on the ease of the Qur'an. We understand from this surah that the Qur'an does not bring difficulty in understanding unless we cause it to be difficult. It was revealed as an authority and a guide that is easy to understand and easy to remember. What, then, is our excuse for abandoning it?

The end of Surah Qaf, along with much of Surah At Tur, tells us about the Day of *Qiyamah* and the life to come. These surahs remind us that no one can escape death and each soul will be accountable for itsevery action. We are reminded in these verses of the chaotic scene on that Day. There will be no option of turning away and Heaven and Hell will be brought forth for people to enter. As is explained in Surah Adh Dhariyat, those who do not believe in the *Akhirah* will be confronted with the greatest of signs, and each will be accountable for what they denied. Surah At Tur tells us that people of Hell will ask if it is only an illusion or if it is real. They will be in shock at the reality of it. Paradise, on the other hand, is described as a place of happiness and socialization. Surah At Tur ends with Allah (swt) questioning the logic of those who reject. He has explained the destination of those who reject and has pointed out His many signs throughout these surahs . He will ask them if they created anything from nothing. Did they really think their knowledge was greater than Allah (swt)?

Surah Adh Dhariyat ends with a reminder to us of the purpose of our creation. We were made for no other reason than to worship Allah (swt). Therefore, there is no act pleasing to Allah (swt) that we engage in that is not an act of worship. If we help our parents, that is an act of worship. If we help our spouses and are patient with our children, these are acts of worship. Though they are responsibilities on us as well, Allah (swt) gives us rewards for fulfilling them.

The whole world is a place of worship, and every hour of our lives is the time for worship. We must reflect on how we spend our time worshipping Allah (swt). Are we worshipping Allah (swt) when we are watching TV in the middle of the night? Are we worshipping Allah (swt) when we are spending countless hours visiting site after site on the Internet without purpose? Allah (swt) is telling us that we should always be worshipping Him by using every moment of our time, regardless of where we are, by engaging in actions pleasing to Him.

The Qur'an is a gift that never ceases to grant us something new and rewarding each time we open it. Let us not then make it a decoration piece on our shelves. May Allah fill our hearts with love for Him (swt), love for our Prophet (peace be upon him), and love for His (swt) book.

Exercises for Surah Qaf, Adh Dhariyat, At Tur, Al Qamar

---

1. Remember the consequences of the transgressing civilizations before our own. What are you doing to make sure you are not like them in their errors?
2. The Qur'an is not difficult. Take understanding the Qur'an one step at a time. Start with basic classes that teach you how to understand concepts of the Qur'an. The *seerah* is the context in which the Qur'an was revealed. One cannot completely understand the Qur'an without understanding the life of the Prophet (peace be upon him)and the culture of the *Jahiliya* Arabs.
3. Remember the purpose of your life on earth. Allah(swt)has created humans for worship. Do not be overwhelmed by this verse. It does not mean that a person must stand in prayer for the entirety of his or her life. Or even that their life will be judged soley on

166

how long they stood in prayer. Worship can be done in many other forms. All things pleasing to Allah (swt) are forms of worship. Write down ten things that you can do in addition to extra prayers that fill your days with acts of worship. Some examples are:

a. Spend extra time with parents, even when you do not need anything from them or they from you.

b. Play games with your children or do activities with them that make them happy.

c. Do something for someone less fortunate than you. Assist them with their needs or make them a meal.

d. Sit down and listen to the recitation of Qur'an for a few minutes a day.

Surahs Ar Rahman, Al Waqiah, Al Hadid (55, 56, 57)

These three surahs discuss the common theme of Allah's greatness, the Day of Resurrection, and Paradise. Both Surah Ar Rahman's and Surah Al Hadid's opening verses establish the greatness of Allah (swt). Rahman is one of Allah's greatest names, one with which He is most often referred. It serves as a reminder to us that, above so many other attributes, our Lord, Allah (swt), is unfailingly merciful to His (swt) servants. Similarly, Surah Al Hadid opens with examples of His (swt) power by describing the creation of the heavens and the earth. In the early verses in this surah He (swt) reminds us of the universal truth that all things will in the end return to Allah (swt). We are also reminded in Surahs Waqiah and Rahman of the inability of humans to resist His power and His plan. As such, Surah Ar Rahman and Surah Al Waqiah return us, at the end of each surahof them, to a declaration of the Glory and Might of Allah (swt). He is reminding us that if we remember these attributes of Him, we will be better equipped to navigate our way through the trials of life because we would remember to put our trust in Allah (swt). In remembering His attributes, we will make decisions in this life that will lead to enjoyment in the life to come.

These surahs also provide us with unique descriptions of the Resurrection and the Afterlife. Surah Ar Rahman takes us on a journey from the creation of man and *jinn* to the moment when all things on earth will perish, and then to the resurrection and judgment. Through these surahs we are given a detailed description of Paradise. Surah Ar Rahman tells us about the endless fountains and the fruits. It describes the beautiful furniture of Paradise as green cushions and elegant carpets. Surah Al Waqiah elaborates on the drinks that will be brought forth in cups of gold. No inhabitant of Paradise will need to exert any effort to obtain it; they will simply desire to have a drink and it will be served to them. The inhabitants of Paradise will enjoy such services as they sit reclined on thrones. They will be young in age and never will hear an ill word. They will delight themselves with all the fruits and drinks they desire and will have the constant comfort of the shade to relax. These are the descriptions of this beautiful place that Allah (swt) has shown us in Surah Al Waqiah. Allah (swt) has promised such a reward to those who do good in this life. Why then do we allow ourselves to be sidetracked by the pleasures of this world?

The pleasures of this world are nothing compared to the description of *Jannah*. In the early verses of Surah Al Waqiah, Allah (swt) gives examples of the favors He has bestowed upon us: the water, rain, energy, fire, trees and herbs. He has provided us these favors and signs so that we may dwell on and work toward the *Akhirah*, not that we busy ourselves with only the temporary things in this world. In Surah Ar Rahman, Allah (swt) presents a strong challenge to the reader. He provides us with examples of His favors in so many verses of the Qur'an, and thenHe poses the question: "Which of the favors of your Lord will you deny?" He has sent so many favors, so many blessings, and so many signs; which one will we reject? We should ask ourselves: do we really appreciate and show gratitude for every blessing in our bodies, in our intellect, and in our spirit? Do we recognize the blessing of sight, hearing, and feeling? Which favors are we neglectful of attributing to Him (swt)? Allah (swt) knows that we are not conscious of all of His favors, so He poses the question 31 times throughout Surah Ar Rahman. He is emphasizing the extreme importance of reflecting on each sign and recognizing it as a creation of Allah.

In Surah Al Hadid, Allah (swt) makes mention of a specific blessings that has been granted to us, and that is the blessing of wealth. In verses 7-9, we understand that Allah (swt) tests us with that which we love. In order to attain Paradise that He so beautifully describes in the two previous surahsurahs, we need to sacrifice out of the things that are dear to us. Allah (swt) asks who will give Him the best loan so that He may multiply it and provide Paradise as a reward. We see through these examples the insignificance of this present life, except to race for doing good and attaining Paradise.

Let us work on becoming more generous in Ramadan as Allah (swt) is more generous in Ramadan than any other month.

Exercises for Surah Ar Rahman, Al Waqiah, Al Hadid

---

1. Reflect on the Day of Resurrection and the Mercy of Allah (swt). If you want His Mercy on the Day of Judgment, make sure you engage in things that are pleasing to Him as a way of indicating that.
2. Learn some of the names of Allah (swt) and study how He manifests those characteristics in the world.
3. Go back to your list of descriptions of Heaven and Hell from one of the previous exercises; add the description of Paradise from Surah Waqiah to your list. Imagine yourself in such a place, with everything your heart desires. Make a commitment now to add or remove one specific thing from your life whichwill take youanother step closer to getting there.

Surahs Al Mujadilah, Al Hashr, Al Mumtahanah (58, 59, 60)

Surah Al Mujadilah talks about the importance of being mindful of our speech as it can destroy families and communities. It begins with the story of a man who verbally abused his wife. Allah (swt) draws our attention in this verse to His ability to hear the speech of every servant, even what is said in private. This verse also establishes the rights of the women. Allah (swt)explainedthe relationship between husband and wife, making it clear that such treatment would not be tolerated. An example of the destruction ill speech can have is also seen when the disbelievers express their animosity toward the Prophet (peace be upon him).

Surah Al Hashr talks about the hypocrites—*Bani Nadhir*tribe in Madinah—who violated the peace treaty by plotting against the Prophet (peace be upon him). They thought no one on the side of the Prophet (peace be upon him) could hear their plots and plans, but Allah (swt) hears all things said in open and in secret. Allah (swt) reminds us in verses 8 and 9 of Surah Mujadilah that secret counsel should not be held for reasons of hostility; rather, it could be held for righteous matters and self-restraint. This is a reminder to us to be conscious of our words as every word that we speak will be recorded and will come back to us as weight on our scale toward good or bad. Which side of our scale are our words falling on? It is in Surahs Mujadilah and Hashr that Allah (swt) addresses the rising of the hypocrites and the severe consequences they face as a result of their deception. As the animosity against the Prophet and the Muslims increased, Allah (swt) directed the Muslims not to be discouraged.

Allah (swt) reminds us in Surah Al Hashr that communities are built on love, harmony, good speech, and trusted leadership. He (swt) reminds us of the beautiful example of the *Muhajireen* and the *Ansar* as is explained in Surah Hashr, verses 8-10. The *Ansar* exemplified love and kindness by giving

170

half of what they owned to strangers, the *Muhajireen*. Surah Al Mumtahanahdescribes these two types of people Allah (swt) has given as examples, and commands us never to haveas friends those who will take us away from Allah (swt). They will only dragus with them as they pave their own path to Allah's wrath. Rather, we should moveourselves into the company of those who do good. Such friends one should hold with both hands, as they will enable us to pave our own path to Allah's Mercy and Forgiveness. This is not to say that we cannot have friends who have different beliefs, but we cannot take as friends those who prevent us from worshipping Allah (swt) or those who push us toward what Allah (swt) has forbidden. We must also remember that regardless of the belief of the people we interact with, we must follow the example of our beloved Prophet (peace be upon him) to always meet people with kindness and gentleness.

Allah (swt) reminds us in Surah Mumtahanah that those we take as friends, good or bad, will not be able to help us on the Day of Judgment. They can influence us in this life as to which path we will take. Ramadan is a time of reflection and evaluation. Let us reflect on the company we keep: do we have friends who will bring us closer to Allah?

Exercises for Surah Al Mujadilah, Al Hashr, Al Mumtahanah

1. Be mindful of your speech in public and in private. Hurtful words are no better then hurtful actions but much easier to engage in. All of us make mistakes and say things, from time to time, that we may not mean. Make a goal to spend the next week, being very aware of every word that you speak. Spend a moment before you start talking to think if you are choosing the best and kindest words. Always respond to harsh words with kindness and remember Allah (swt) hears the

171

conversation. Pay particular attention to how you speak to your parents, spouses and children.

2. Try to have the generosity and the love that the *Ansar* had for the *Muhajireen*. They saw their brothers and sisters struggling and, without hesitation, shared half of their possessions. If you meet a brother or sister who has nothing, give what you know you can. Remember that Allah (swt) replenishes people for their generosity and remember the spirit of the Ansar.

3. Reflect on the company you keep. Are these the kind of people who lead you towards or away from Allah (swt)?

Surahs As Saff, Al Jumu'ah, Al Munafiqun, At Taghabun (61, 62, 63, 64)

Allah (swt) calls mankind to heed the warning brought by His Messenger and His book. Allah (swt) is telling the people of Arabia to take the Divine revelation seriously. He is reminding mankind to take the Qur'an seriously just as He asked us to take the Torah seriously. In this surah, He calls the believers to back up their words with action. This is a very powerful reminder to us in an environment and time where the practice of religion is challenged by the unfortunate norms of society. as Muslims we cannot lay a claim to Islam only by verbal commitment but that we must practice the faith as well.

Islam is about putting our words into action. Allah (swt) commands us to dress, speak, and behave and so forth in certain manners. We must obey those commands in addition to verbally proclaiming our commitment to Allah (swt). In verse 8 of Surah As Saff, Allah (swt) talks about the disbelievers responding to the words of Allah (swt).[67] They responded with their own words trying to suppress the light of Allah's book.

---

[67] Their intention is to extinguish Allah's Light (by blowing) with their mouths: But Allah will complete (the revelation of) His Light, even though the Unbelievers may detest (it).

Those who rejected faith had only the ability to reject it by words. As we read in Surah Ad Dukhan, the *Quraysh* sought the supplication of the Prophet (peace be upon him) to bring rain down in a time of drought and they were granted rain. Such actions of the rejecters of the Prophet (peace be upon him) affirmed the truth of Islam. Similarly, Surah Al Jumu'ah shows us the example of the Prophet (peace be upon him) applying the message in his own life, not just preaching it for others to follow. If the most perfect of men—a man who belongs in the highest level of paradise—never compromised a command of Allah (swt) and never found it sufficient to only speak and not follow with action, why then do we allow ourselves that leniency? His place in paradise waspromised yet he acted upon every word he preached. This is a strong reminder to us that we must do the same.

Allah (swt) provides us with yet another powerful metaphor of the donkey that carries books on his back, unable to do anything with them. Such is the person who has the book of Allah (swt) and does not benefit from it. This is also emphasized throughout Surah Al Munafiqun that our actions should reflect what we are saying. At the same time, this surah reminds us that judgment should be left to Allah (swt).

In Surah As Saff, verses 10 and 11, Allah (swt) explains the best type of trade is the trade with Allah (swt), using our money and our wealth and possessions in His way and in the way of His Prophet (peace be upon him). That is better use of our wealth than any other type of financial dealing. Unfortunately, some of us hold the need for money so close to our hearts that we neglect the obligation to separate ourselves from it during the Jummah prayer time.

It is in Surah Al Jumu'ah that we see the command from Allah (swt) to leave business in order to attend Jummah. This was revealed to us when the Prophet (peace be upon him) was conducting the Jummah prayer and some of the followers stood

173

up and left in order to attend to the business that came to town. Today, this is relevant to us, as most Muslims do not have holiday on Fridays. It is then essentialthen that we make sure to attend the congregational prayer by whatever means necessary. Leaving business behind includes turning off our cell phones and other modes of communication in order to directour full focus into our prayer. This is necessary in both the Jumu'ah prayer and any other prayer. After all, is there any person who might try to contact us superior or more loved than the One we are praying to? Verses 10 and 11 of Surah Al Jumu'ah remind us that it is good to engage in business in order to sustain our families and ourselves but the best business is with our Lord.

This is also stated in Surah Al Munafiqun. Allah (swt) reminds us that the material world can be a means to attaining Paradise. Therefore, we should not completely abandon the desire to attain some wealth. We should not sit at home while our families are living in difficulty and discomfort and wait for Allah (swt) to provide for us. He reminds us that business and other such work is a means for sustenance and enjoyment of the worldly life, but it should be done in moderation. Allah (swt) asks us several times throughout the Qur'an to sacrifice luxuries of this life for the eternal luxury of the next. In this surah, He is balancing it with an explanation that spending to make your family happy, to provide them sufficient food and clothing, to provide them with an environment that is emotionally and spiritually beneficial for them, is a means for attaining a healthy and comfortable home in *Jannah*. Surah At Taghabun explains this by telling us money and children are a test for us. Tests are not only "bad"—these verses do not indicate that our children are created as a difficulty for us, so we should not deal withthem as such. Rather, these versesaresaying that they are a trust that Allah (swt) has placed in our hands and it is how carefully and thoughtfully we deal withthem that will determine our success.

We must remember that whatever the test, we should not

trade anything inthis limited life on earth at the expense of the eternal next life.

Exercises for Surah As Saff, Al Jumu'ah, Al Munafiqun, At Taghabun

1. Proclaim your faith with your words *and* actions. Remember that being Muslim isnot only by proclaiming the creed but also by adhering to the commands and prohibitions of Allah (swt) and His Messenger.
2. Go to Jummah prayer each week and take your children with you. Do what you can to make arrangements atwork even if you have to start early on Friday or end your day later.
3. Reflect on money and children as tests of trust that Allah (swt) has placed withyou. What are we doing to make sure we secure these two trusts as instruments to attain paradise?

Surahs At Talaq and At Tahrim (65, 66)

SurahsAt Talaq and At Tahrim talk about the status and rights of women in Islam. Surah *Talaq*, divorce, was revealed as a result of the treatment of divorced women at the hands of pre-Islamic Arabs. Women who divorced had no rights once separated from their husbands and were often ill-treated. Surah At Talaq changed that situation by teaching Muslims how to appropriately deal with divorces, including the details of divorcing and maintaining the needs of the women after a divorce. It also addresses the issues of child support and custody, matters that were previously unheard of.

Surah At Tahrim continues by giving the example of how to appropriately handle relationships with one's spouse. The Prophet of Allah (peace be upon him) is used as an example. We are given examples in the Qur'an of the types of difficulties that

175

he faced in his marriage, showing the human side of the Prophet. He was the most perfect human being, but was not exempt from tests in his personal life. This is a reminder to us that our marriages are not doomed when we hit times of trouble or disputes. It is only a test of how we handle these challenges.

We should also take from his example that in all the stories regarding tension in hismarriage, the Prophet (peace be upon him) never made it acceptable to verbally, physically, or emotionally abuse his wife. Rather, he handled matters of dispute with kindness, gentleness, patience and wisdom, including seeking mediation when needed.

Exercises forAt Talaq and At Tahrim

1. Make yourself familiar with the stories of Prophet Muhammad (peace be upon him) and the situations in which he had difficulties in his relationships with his wives. Remember his kindness and patience when dealing with your own disputes in marriage.
2. If separation ever becomes necessary, treat each other with dignity and kindness.
3. Remind yourself daily that Prophet Muhammad (peace be upon him) never resorted to verbally, physically, or emotionally abusing his wife.
4. Seek mediation when needed in your relationship.

Surahs Al Mulk, Al Qalam, Al Haqqah, Al Ma'arij (67, 68, 69, 70)

Surah Al Mulk is recited as a protection from the punishment of the grave. Allah (swt) describes His power in this surah. He tells us of the entire universe being in His hands and that He has power over everything in it. He is the Creator and the Sustainer of it all. Surah Al Mulk, along with Surah Al Qalam and Surah Al Haqqah, describes the Day of Resurrection and the regret that the wrongdoers will feel on that day. In Surah Al Qalam Allah (swt) warns us against compromising our principles in this life because such compromises may be at the expense of the Hereafter. We are reminded that we will stand before Allah (swt) on that Day and we will be made accountable for our deeds in this life. Allah (swt) reminds us of a story in Surah Al 'Isra' in which two young people owned a garden that was previously owned by their father. The father of the young boys maintained the garden and dispersed the profit to the poor. The young men decided to hold the profit for themselves, taking the garden for granted. Allah (swt) removed all the vegetation of the garden while they slept, reminding them of who provides bounties for us on earth. We are reminded in these surahs that Allah (swt) brings sustenance and it is maintained through gratitude and sharing with others. Humanity is called upon through these surahs to share the resources that we have with each other and not to be stingy. When we give, we should give knowing that Allah (swt) sees our generosity and increases for us what we share. And when we find ourselves withholding what Allah (swt) has blessed us with, we should remember the story of the garden that stopped giving a harvest.

Similar to Surah Al Haqqah, Surah Al Ma'arij talks about creation and belief. As Allah (swt) gives a description of *Qiyamah* in Surah Al Haqqah, Surah Al Ma'arij questions those who do not believe in that Day. It reaffirms the belief in the life to come and explains the consequences of *Qiyamah* for the wrongdoers after they question the penalty of their actions. Allah (swt) is showing them the reality of that Day as *Qiyamah* is one of the most difficult aspects of belief. There are those that do not believe, those whobelieve butact as if they do not believe, and those whoknow and use it as a guide for their every action. Which of these are we? Surah Al Ma'arij also discusses the reality of time.We feel like this life is so long, but the reality is that it is but a brief moment and the *Qiyamah* that we so often forget, is right around the corner. As the Prophet (peace be upon him) tells us "Heaven and Hell are closer to you than the sandals of your shoes". Allah (swt) reminds us in this beautiful surah of the hope that we should have in Allah (swt). He gives a beautiful description of those who will be saved from the punishment of Hell Fire and the portrayl of the inhabitants of Paradise. May Allah (swt) make us among those people.

Exercises forAl Mulk, Al Qalam, Al Haqqah, Al Ma'arij

1. When you feel like withholding what Allah (swt) has given you, remember the story of the two brothers and the garden that stopped giving harvest.
2. Make it a habit to commit the first check you write each month to charity. Even if the amount is small, write it before paying any bills or other spending.
3. For the youth that are in college or younger, set aside time each month to use the resources that Allah has blessed you with, time and energy, for a charitable cause. As you complete that task each month, remember the *hadith*, "Heaven and Hell are closer to you than the sandals of your shoes". Be proud of your work in helping others.

Surah Nuh (71)

Surah Nuh talks about Prophet Nuh's (may Allah be pleased with him) call to his people. Allah explains that Prophet Nuh was sent as a messenger to warn mankind. He began his invitation by giving them glad tidings and motivated them to seek forgiveness from Allah (swt).

This surah shows the exceptional effort of Prophet Nuh in calling his people to Allah (swt). He called his people day and night but the more he invited them, the more they turned their backs and refused. This was a challenge for the Prophet because of the level of arrogance of the people. He called publicly and privately and used every means to help them find their way to Allah (swt), but they continuously rejected because they wanted to follow their whims and desires. This is a lesson to us that, though the odds may be against us, we need to continue on our course to Allah (swt) and attainment of His pleasure. The pressures and challenges that we face are not excuses for turning our backs on Allah (swt), the One who has given us everything that we possess.

Surah Nuh teaches us a great lesson in patience; one of the greatest examples on this topic. Allah (swt) reminds us that Prophet Nuh (peace be upon him) was not calling people to Allah (swt) for 10, 20, 50, or a 100 years. The mission of Prophet Nuh, (peace be upon him) was 950 years long! And throughout this time Nuh (peace be upon him) was mocked and strongly challenged even by his own family. Despite the length in which he endured this test from Allah (swt), his commitment did not waiver. He continuously made *dua* to Allah (swt) for help and guidance. He sought forgiveness as a means for attaining nearness to Allah (swt) and the strength and ability to continue in his mission. How is it that we question Allah (swt) when we do not see the answer to our supplication after a week or a month?

The Prophet of Allah waited 950 years. At the end of 950 years, Allah (swt) conveyed to His prophet that no others would believe. He had completed his work and the promise of Allah (swt) would come into fruition upon those who rejected the Message. It was only after that knowledge that Prophet Nuh (peace be upon him)supplicated to Allah to show his people the reality of Allah (swt). It is important for us to know and remember that Nuh (may Allah be pleased with him), after 950 years, did not give up on doing what Allah had commanded him to do; he only concluded his mission when Allah (swt) told him it was over.

None of us will live to see the 950th year of our life, so we know that Allah (swt) will not test us as greatly as the test of Prophet Nuh (peace be upon him), but we must take a lesson

179

from his example of extraordinary patience. We must remember that Allah is All Hearing, All Seeing, and He will not neglect to respond to anyone's supplication. We must remember that the response to our *du'a* will come in different forms at different times. It may not come in exactly the manner we hoped and planned. We need to establish this knowledge within our hearts and, if we do that, patience and ease will follow.

Exercises for Surah Nuh

1. The next time someone talks to you about Islam, reflect on how much patience you have with them. If you find it difficult to have patience in these situations, think about the patience of Prophet Nuh (may Allah be pleased with him) and what you can do to grow closer to his level of patience.
2. When you feel that someone around you is a test for you, make *dua* for him or her as Nuh (May Allah be pleased with him) made *dua* for the help and guidance of those who mocked him.
3. Have patience in making *dua*. Every time you make *dua*, remind yourself that Allah responds to every *dua* in His time.
4. Never give up on doing good, regardless of what the results of your work appear to be. Nuh (may Allah be pleased with him), strived to help his people for 950 years, never giving up until Allah (swt) gave him permission to do so.

Surahs Al Jinn (72)

Surah Al Jinn was revealed to the Prophet Muhammad (peace be upon him) after the events of *Ta'if*. The people did not listen to the call of the Prophet (peace be upon him), but Allah (swt) made the *jinns* listen. This served as a comfort that, though the people rejected the message, the *jinns* accepted it. This surah brings up a topic which many people are uneasy discussing. But we should realize that *jinns*, like humans, are of two kinds: the believing and the non-believing (*Iblis* of course being one of the non-believing).

Reciting *Ayatul Kursi* after each prayer and before sleep will serve as a shield between human and *jinn*. We should remember to avoid obsessing over the issue of *jinn*, as sometimes the problem a person is facing is actually a mental health factor. We must look at the source before the solution. Not all the phenomena of the Unseen can be explained, but Allah (swt) has told us they do, in fact, exist. This surah tells us about the story of Suleiman and his interactions with *jinn*. It also summarizes the power of *jinn*.

The later part of this surah discusses the purpose of the *masjid* in the life of the Muslim community. It serves as a place for remembrance of Allah (swt), a place where people find sanctuary and know one another based on their love for Allah (swt). It is a place where people work to improve both the human and the spiritual aspect of their lives. Is this what we use our *masjid* for, or is it only a place we visit in Ramadan, upon news of a death, or for *Eid*?

The *masjid* should be a regular part of our lives and should serve as a sanctuary to bring us closer to Allah (swt). It should not be an emotionally distant place that we only visit a handful of times a year. As we close off this Ramadan, we should make a commitment to bring our families and ourselves closer to the house of Allah (swt), even if it is just once a week for one prayer. This will help each of us to maintain the spiritual connection to Allah (swt) that Ramadan brings.

---

1. Do not allow yourself to obsess over *jinns* and understand that they are a different creation of Allah (swt).
2. Make the *masjid* a part of your weekly, if not daily, routine as a way to maintain a spiritual connection with Allah (swt) and with the community throughout the year.

Muzzamil, Al Muddathir (73, 74)

Allah (swt) places great importance on exercising patience in Surah Nuh. This theme continues through the surahs that follow it. Allah (swt) also talks in Surah Al Muzammil about the wife of the Prophet, Khadijah (may Allah be pleased with her), who was a source of his patience. She provided him an environment of comfort during his time of distress in the beginning of his prophethood. This shows us that while we as individuals must be patient in our trials, support is necessary and should be an active effort from each family member. The trials that take place in the lives of others are a test for them, but they are also a test for us. If a family member is struck by a calamity, it is a test for the rest of the family as to how they will respond to help that person. Khadijah exemplified this by comforting her husband and reminding him of the goodness of his heart. Allah also tells us as individuals how we must look for the strength for patience. Shortly after Angel *Jibreel's* visit to the Prophet (peace be upon him), Allah (swt) revealed in Surah Al Muzammil the command to stand up at night in prayer. Allah (swt) was preparing him for the difficult mission that was ahead. This is a lesson to us that, in times of trial and difficulty, we should connect more with Allah (swt). He is always available for us to turn to Him and He is telling us how and when to do it: in prayer and in the later part of the night.

Allah (swt) reminds us throughout the Qur'an that it is

in his remembrance that our hearts find ease. He invites us to it in times of good but He has provided this as a medicine for our times of difficulty. This was the Prophet's preparation to face the world. We too can benefit from a dose of it each morning before we go out to face ours. Surah Al Muddathir continues the theme of patience by relating the Prophet's frightening event of witnessing Angel Jibreel in his true form for the first time. Angel Jibreel encompassed the whole horizon on a hanging seat that was between the heaven and earth. This was the time of declaration of the message, and was one of the most overwhelming events for the Prophet Muhammad (peace be upon him).

Surah Muddathir also reminds us of other situations in which the Prophet of Allah required an immense amount of patience. We should reflect on each of these and ask ourselves if we had been tested with the same type of trials, what would be our level of patience? Our beloved Prophet Muhammad (peace be upon him) had his feet stoned at *Ta'if*, his teeth knock out in *Uhud*, and the insides of animals thrown on his back when he made *sujjud*. He was called names, laughed at, mocked, and his family faced serious false accusations. But through all of this, he did not question Allah (swt). He maintained patience and was a source of helping others maintain patience, even when the action was against him. This is a clear emphasis on the importance of not allowing anger and emotion to take us away from our focus being on Allah (swt).

Exercises for Surahs Al Muzzamil, Al Muddathir

1. Examine how you respond when people around you are struck by calamity. Do the tests they go through bring you to respond in a caring and humble manner or are you finding yourself acting arrogant when others rather than you are tested in this way?

2. Look at how Khadijah (may Allah be pleased with her) responded to the tests that the Prophet of Allah(peace be upon him) faced throughout their time together.
3. Choose a book on the life of the Prophet (peace be upon him), and read about the struggles he faced at *Ta'if*. Remember these are the things he endured to leave the message for all the generations that followed him.

Al Qiyamah, Al Insan, Al Mursalat (75, 76, 77)

Surah Al Insan begins with a question that humbles us by bringing us back to the moment when we were nothing. This state of being nothing is referring to the time before conception (also mentioned at the end of Surah Al Qiyamah). Surah Al Insan also talks about the two paths of humanity but reminds us that there is only one path that is compatible with the mission of human beings which is explained in these verses. Allah compares the Hereafter of those who are grateful in this life and those who are ungrateful in this life. Surah Al Insan gives a very moving description of sweetness of Paradise.

Surah Al Mursalat talks about the people who distance themselves from thoughts of the *Qiyamah* because they do not want to restrict their worldly pleasures by working within the guidelines decreed by Allah (swt). They do not want to forgo their pleasure in this life, but they do not realize that Allah (swt) is calling them to a greater and everlasting pleasure. He has given us these descriptions of Heaven and Hell so that we can reflect on which one we would like to spend our lives working toward. We should reflect on these descriptions each morning and each night. Such reminders will allow us to guide our daily actions to being those that bring us closer to Jannah. Each evening we can reflect on where our actions place us and what actions we need to change.

Exercises for Surah Al Qiyamah, Al Insan, Al Mursalat

---

1. Evaluate the worldy pleasures in your life. Which ones are at the expense of the Afterlife? Think about what you can do to reduce and eliminate those things that are at the expense of the Afterlife.
2. Each morning use the descriptions provided in these surahs. Allow these descriptions to help guide you to the activities that will bring you closer to Allah.

Juz 'Amma Part 1 – Surah An Naba through Surah Al Layl (78 through 92)

Surah An Naba and Surah An Naziat provide us with detailed descriptions of the shock and the enjoyment of people at the Day of Judgment.

Verses 17-40 of Surah An Naba cover the events of *Qiyamah* and the description of Paradise and Hellfire. Likewise, Surah An Naziat also addresses this in verses 43-46. In addition, Surah An Naziat provides us with a reminder of the nations that came before us, including the stories of Musa and Pharaoh. The end of Surah An Naziat, and Surah An Naba describe how people attain Paradise. Allah (swt) reminds us that, while people question the reality of that Day, no one will be able to deny the reality of the *Akhirah* when the veil over it is removed and a window to the next life will be revealed.

Surah Abasa begins by talking about the incident of the blind man who came to the Prophet (peace be upon him) seeking guidance. This event was a lesson and was also considered to be the first "disability act", as it empowered a blind man and highlighted the importance of the contributions of each and every person to our communities. It also calls our attention to the reality of death and that each of us will be

185

placed beneath the earth's dirt with nothing but our deeds to help us.

Surah At Takwir then discusses the situation before the Resurrection, including the collapse of the sun, the falling of the stars, the crumbling of the mountains, and the burning of the ocean. These are proofs that Allah's promise is true and that we will in fact be held accountable for our actions. While these events will serve as evidence of the reality of the Judgment, the Day itself will not be the time for us to change our ways. We must remind ourselves of these events and live each day of our lives as if those events could happen at any moment. These early surahs of Juz 'Amma deal with the great events of *Qiyamah*.

Surahs Al Infitar and Al Inshiqaq remind us that we are often deceived by the everyday blessings that Allah (swt) has granted us. We forget to thank Him for our ears, eyes, and sense of touch every morning. We forget to thank Him each day that we have our health. We must be grateful for these blessings by only using them in ways that are pleasing to Him. We are reminded that no human can help one another on the Day of Judgment, so we must be mindful each day of preparing our souls to stand before Allah (swt) with no assistance other than our deeds. Abusing our blessings by making them a means of sin will require us to face the consequence of those actions. Only those who believe and do righteous deeds will be spared. Allah (swt) has reminded us of all these things and then poses the question of why we do not prostrate to Allah after recognizing His blessings upon us. This is something we should ask ourselves when we are slow in attending to our prayers or other obligations. What could possibly warrant our reluctance in showing gratitude and praise to Him (swt)?

Surah Al Mutaffifin is a Makkan surah that begins with a warning to those who commit injustice. There are those who demand their rights and ask for exact measures, but when others seek their rights, they are slow to give or give less than what is due. Allah (swt) connects actions with accountability and the *Akhirah*. He talks about two categories of people: those who will enjoy themselves in the life to come and those who made fun and mockery of believers and, as a result, will face the punishment in the life to come.

Surah Al Buruj continues the theme of fighting injustice. It addresses those who try to restrict freedom of religion. Allah (swt) relates the story of the patience and perseverance of the believers. The believing men and women had to exhibit great levels of tolerance and patience as they faced persecution and trials in their faith. It ends with examples of those who committed grave injustices—such as Pharoah and *Thamud*—and the ramifications of those transgressions.

Surah At Tariq is a Makkan surah that draws our attention to the phenomenon of the stars and the great creation of Allah (swt). It humbles us and reminds us of our beginnings. It serves as a great reminder of Allah's power over all things and that no one can overcome the power and decrees of Allah Almighty.

Surah Al A'la is a beautiful Makkan surah that begins by underlining Allah's Majesty and the importance of *Wahy* and the revelation of the Qur'an. It declares that only people who adhere and listen to the message will benefit from it. Surah Al A'la addresses an important issue of self-purification, the objective of every Muslim, particularly as we read the Qur'an in this blessed month of Ramadan. As we fast in the day and pray at night, we should strive to become closer to Allah (swt) and work towards purifying ourselves.

Surah Al Ghashiya is another Makkan surah that deals with two important issues. First, it covers the *Qiyamah* and its great events, including the contrasting experiences of those who prepared themselves for that Day and those who did not. Secondly, this surah talks about the greatness of Allah (swt) and gives examples of His greatness in His creations. It shows that all of the creations we see and those that we do not see, point to the Oneness and Greatness of Allah Almighty.

Surah Al Fajris a Makkan surah whose beautiful verses draw our attention to another great phenomenon: the breaking of the dawn. It mentions the importance of the days of *Dhul Hijjah* and the 10 nights by which Allah (swt) swears in these verses. He talks about the stories of the nations that deny the Messengers of Allah, such as people of *'Ad, Thamud*, and Pharaoh: "Have you not seen what your Lord has done with the people of *'Ad*?" The other aspect speaks of the law of Allah (swt) in testing humanity by giving itblessings and opportunities or by testing them with calamities. The surah concludes by speaking about the different categories of people on the Day of Resurrection and the ending of the universe as we know it.

Surah Al Fajr is followed by the Makkan surah, Surah Al Balad. It begins with the mentioning of the Holy city of Makkah to draw attention to the importance of the Prophet (peace be upon him) as a dweller of that city. The surah gives the indication that the Prophet (peace be upon him) has the right to live in Makkah, and reminds the disbelievers that one of the greatest sins in the eyes of Allah (swt) is to harm the Prophet of Allah (peace be upon him), particularly in the blessed city of Makkah, a place that is supposed to be a place of security and refuge.

Surah Al Balad talks about the people of Makkah, the disbelievers who bragged about their power and rejected Prophet Muhammad (peace be upon him). They expended their wealth in an effort to stop the Prophet (peace be upon him) from conveying the message. It then concludes by speaking about the difficulty that people will face on The Day of Judgment and the reward and punishment that will be determined for each individual.

Then the Qur'an draws attention in Surah Ash Shams to another phenomenon—the sun, which we need to maintain life on earth, yet take for granted every day. Allah (swt) swears by seven things in this surah: the sun, the moon, the day, the night, the sky, the earth, and the soul.

Surah Al Layl talks about the choices humans make in choosing a path in life. It begins by swearing by night and other natural phenomena. Allah (swt) establishes that human beings may strive for different objectives and desires in this life, but Allah (swt) gives examples of those who strive for good. Those who give are generous, believe in the life to come and are sincere in their actions. Paradise is their abode. Those who hold back and live without heeding to the commands and limitations decreed by Allah (swt)—for them are consequences for their disobedience. This surah teaches sincerity and devotion and calls us to be devoted and sincere in our actions and efforts.

Exercises for Juz 'Amma Part 1

1. Learn from Surah Abasa that we have to accommodate the needs, and encourage the participation, of the disabled in our communities.
2. Show gratitude to Allah (swt) by utilizing your senses in the proper way. Let your eyes see, your ears hear, and your mouths taste what is permissible, and let your hands touch what is pure.
3. In all of your relationships be just. Do not demand from someone more than you give. And never betray another person's trust.
4. Speak up against persecution of religious minorities. Do not sit in silence when places of worship are destroyed, or genocide or bigotry is evident.
5. Establish a consistent daily *dhikr* routine.
6. Study history and human behavior to understand the people of the past. Connect this knowledge to what you learn in the Qur'an.
7. Evaluate where the bulk of your time is spent and if that fits with your objectives in life.

Juz 'Amma Part 2 - Surah Ad Duha through Surah An Nas (93 through 114)

Juz 'Amma contains the surahs that deal with the signs of Allah (swt) and invites humanity to heed that call. Surah Ad Duha and Surah Al Inshirah bring comfort to us as Muslims. Surah Ad Duha is a surah that inspires hope within the heart of the believer as it was revealed after a long pause in revelation. Angel *Jibreel* had not visited the Prophet (peace be upon him)for some time. It reaffirmed for the Prophet Muhammad (peace be upon him) that Allah (swt) had not abandoned or forsaken him. This is also a sign to us of the nearness of Allah (swt) to His servant. He was aware of the distress that was in the heart of the Prophet (peace be upon him). Allah (swt) knows the feelings that we have in our hearts in times of difficulty—feelings no one else can fully understand. Allah (swt) is reminding us of His infinite knowledge and the comfort He generously provides.

This surah also reminds us to care for the poor and the needy. Ramadan is a time in which all of us have a heightened sense of responsibility to those less fortunate than ourselves. But Ramadan is not a time for action to be followed by months of neglect of responsibilities. Ramadan is a time to train the soul to be active throughout the year. Surah Al Inshirah came as a reminder to the Prophet of Allah's favors upon him. He reminds us how difficult life is and that, after every difficulty, we are promised ease. We must always remain optimistic and look forward to light that follows times of darkness.

Surah At Tin expresses the reminder that the favors of Allah (swt) cover all of humanity. It explains that man has been created in the best of molds. Surah Al 'Alaq brings forth the story of the beginning of the revelation of the Qur'an. The first verses of Surah Al 'Alaq begin the journey of the Prophethood and the message of Islam. It connects knowledge with revelation and attributes human knowledge to Allah Almighty. It also serves as a reminder for us never to be arrogant with our knowledge. In Surah Al Bayyinah, Allah (swt) talks about the purpose of the Qur'an and how it is our criterion of right and wrong for those seeking the guidance and pleasure of Allah (swt).

In Surah Az Zalzalah, Allah (swt) talks about accountability. It means that, regardless of the weight of a bad or good deed, every single deed will fall on one side or the other of our scale. Surah Al 'Adiyat reminds us never to be ungrateful and to be mindful of the limitations placed on the creations of Allah (swt). Like Surah Az Zalzalah, Surah Al 'Adiyat reminds us of our resurrection from our graves. Surah Al Qariah describes what will take place on *Yawm al Qiyamah*. Surah At Takathur warns us not to allow this material world to cost us the joy of the life to come. We are reminded of the reality that we will encounter upon death and the inability to deny it then. Why, then, should we allow ourselves to deny it now?

Surah Al 'Asr is described by Imam Shafi' to be a very powerful surah—one that, if it had been revealed alone, would have been sufficient as it teaches us that all those who engage in things other than faith, good deeds, patience, and perseverance, are truly at loss. Surah Al Humazah and Surah Al Ma'un bring to attention the illusion caused for some people by wealth and power. They mock those less fortunate in material wealth and do not engage in the establishment of justice. Surah Quraysh and Surah Al Fil can be read together, not reciting the *Basmallah* between them (as Surah Al Fil is a continuation of Surah Quraysh). These surahs talk about the saving of the *Ka'bah* and *Makkah* from *Abraha*, and then call people to worship the Lord who protected the *Ka'bah*.

Surah Al Kawthar explains the mocking of the beloved Prophet of Allah (peace be upon him) for fathering only female children. Allah (swt) promises him in this surah that he (peace be upon him) will have something greater than any of those who mock him. He had his beloved daughters in this world, and will have the river of *Kawthar* in *Jannah*. Surah Al Kafirun explains how the Makkans tried to push the Prophet (peace be upon him) in order to force him to compromise his religion in some way. Allah (swt) replied firmly to their efforts declaring that there is no compromise to be made, and people are free to practice the religion they choose, but that, in the end, all will be returned to Allah (swt) for judgment. Surah An Nasr was revealed around the ending of the revelation and the life of our beloved Prophet Muhammad (peace be upon him). Allah (swt) gave the glad tidings of people coming to Islam in large numbers. This was an indication about the end of the message. Surah Al Masad tells the story of a man and his wife who made the spreading of that message as difficult as they could. They tormented the Prophet (peace be upon him) even though he was their own nephew. Surah As Nasr's indication of Muslims coming in numbers shows that the man and wife in Surah Al Masad tried their best to hinder the spread of the message, but Allah's plan was and is above all others.

The final three surahs of the Qur'an—Al Ikhlas, Al Falaq, and An Nas—deal with *Tawhid*. Allah (swt) has given us all the guidance, all the examples, and all the motivation we need to find success. That message is wrapped up with the reminder that, above all, we should hold to the belief of Allah (swt) being One alone, with no partner to be attributed to Him and that His decree is the measure by which to gauge our success. Surah Al Ikhlas equals one third of the Qur'an. Surah Al Falaq and Surah An Nas should be read every night before we sleep.

Exercises for Juz 'Amma Part 2

1. Be optimistic that every time there is a difficulty, ease will follow. Learn the names of Allah and take notice how for every situation in your life there is a name that relates to what you are going through. When you are sick, remember He is the Healer. When you are in

192

financial difficulty, remember He is the Provider and Sustainer. If you have committed sin, He is the Forgiver.

2. As your level of knowledge increases, become more humble. Do not allow your acquisition of knowledge to become something negative by becoming arrogant.
3. Celebrate your accomplishments.

READER'S REFLECTIONS

Conclusion

As this summary comes to an end, we ask Allah (swt) to have us benefit from the Qur'an in Ramadan and to continue to benefit in the months to come. The Qur'an is a book for us to apply to our lives, to adhere to the call, and respond to the order of Allah. As we have shared with you in the month of Ramadan the beautiful surahs of the Qur'an, we need to remember how many times Allah (swt) has said "O you who believe" and "O you people". Our answer should be "Yes. O Allah, whatever You ask of us, You are our Creator and our Sustainer, the One we put our trust in."

O Allah we seek Your Mercy and Forgiveness as this month comes to an end. We have celebrated Your Book and enjoyed our prayers in *qiyam* and *tahajjud*. We ask you to unite our hearts in love for You and for Your Messenger, Muhammad (peace be upon him). We ask you O Allah, to give this community the best in this life and the life to come. We ask you to bring ease and comfort to those who face difficult times. We ask You O Allah to allow us to receive next Ramadan and to guard the good deeds we have established in this Blessed month. O Allah, do not let our relationship with the Qur'an be once a year, rather help us to have an attachment and love for Your words and Your book throughout each day you grant us.

May Allah grant you and your families a Blessed Eid.

List of Qur'anic Verses

1:5 إِيَّاكَ نَعْبُدُ وَإِيَّاكَ نَسْتَعِينُ

2:112 بَلَى مَنْ أَسْلَمَ وَجْهَهُ لِلّهِ وَهُوَ مُحْسِنٌ فَلَهُ أَجْرُهُ عِندَ رَبِّهِ وَلاَ خَوْفٌ عَلَيْهِمْ وَلاَ هُمْ يَحْزَنُونَ

2:143 وَكَذَلِكَ جَعَلْنَاكُمْ أُمَّةً وَسَطًا لِّتَكُونُواْ شُهَدَاء عَلَى النَّاسِ وَيَكُونَ الرَّسُولُ عَلَيْكُمْ شَهِيدًا وَمَا جَعَلْنَا الْقِبْلَةَ الَّتِي كُنتَ عَلَيْهَا إِلاَّ لِنَعْلَمَ مَن يَتَّبِعُ الرَّسُولَ مِمَّن يَنقَلِبُ عَلَى عَقِبَيْهِ وَإِن كَانَتْ لَكَبِيرَةً إِلاَّ عَلَى الَّذِينَ هَدَى اللّهُ وَمَا كَانَ اللّهُ لِيُضِيعَ إِيمَانَكُمْ إِنَّ اللّهَ بِالنَّاسِ لَرَؤُوفٌ رَّحِيمٌ

2:225 لاَّ يُؤَاخِذُكُمُ اللّهُ بِاللَّغْوِ فِيَ أَيْمَانِكُمْ وَلَكِن يُؤَاخِذُكُم بِمَا كَسَبَتْ قُلُوبُكُمْ وَاللّهُ غَفُورٌ حَلِيمٌ

2:282 يَا أَيُّهَا الَّذِينَ آمَنُواْ إِذَا تَدَايَنتُم بِدَيْنٍ إِلَى أَجَلٍ مُّسَمًّى فَاكْتُبُوهُ وَلْيَكْتُب بَّيْنَكُمْ كَاتِبٌ بِالْعَدْلِ وَلاَ يَأْبَ كَاتِبٌ أَنْ يَكْتُبَ كَمَا عَلَّمَهُ اللّهُ فَلْيَكْتُبْ وَلْيُمْلِلِ الَّذِي عَلَيْهِ الْحَقُّ وَلْيَتَّقِ اللّهَ رَبَّهُ وَلاَ يَبْخَسْ مِنْهُ شَيْئًا فَإن كَانَ الَّذِي عَلَيْهِ الْحَقُّ سَفِيهًا أَوْ ضَعِيفًا أَوْ لاَ يَسْتَطِيعُ أَن يُمِلَّ هُوَ فَلْيُمْلِلْ وَلِيُّهُ بِالْعَدْلِ وَاسْتَشْهِدُواْ شَهِيدَيْنِ من رِّجَالِكُمْ فَإِن لَّمْ يَكُونَا رَجُلَيْنِ فَرَجُلٌ وَامْرَأَتَانِ مِمَّن تَرْضَوْنَ مِنَ الشُّهَدَاء أَن تَضِلَّ إْحْدَاهُمَا فَتُذَكِّرَ إِحْدَاهُمَا الأُخْرَى وَلاَ يَأْبَ الشُّهَدَاء إِذَا مَا دُعُواْ وَلاَ تَسْأَمُوْاْ أَن تَكْتُبُوهُ صَغِيرًا أَو كَبِيرًا إِلَى أَجَلِهِ ذَلِكُمْ أَقْسَطُ عِندَ اللّهِ وَأَقْومُ لِلشَّهَادَةِ وَأَدْنَى أَلاَّ تَرْتَابُواْ إِلاَّ أَن تَكُونَ تِجَارَةً حَاضِرَةً تُدِيرُونَهَا بَيْنَكُمْ فَلَيْسَ عَلَيْكُمْ

جُنَاحٌ أَلاَّ تَكْتُبُوهَا وَأَشْهِدُواْ إِذَا تَبَايَعْتُمْ وَلاَ يُضَآرَّ كَاتِبٌ وَلاَ شَهِيدٌ وَإِن تَفْعَلُواْ فَإِنَّهُ فُسُوقٌ

بِكُمْ وَاتَّقُواْ اللهَ وَيُعَلِّمُكُمُ اللهُ وَاللهُ بِكُلِّ شَيْءٍ عَلِيمٌ

2:286 لاَ يُكَلِّفُ اللهُ نَفْسًا إِلاَّ وُسْعَهَا لَهَا مَا كَسَبَتْ وَعَلَيْهَا مَا اكْتَسَبَتْ رَبَّنَا لاَ

تُؤَاخِذْنَا إِن نَّسِينَا أَوْ أَخْطَأْنَا رَبَّنَا وَلاَ تَحْمِلْ عَلَيْنَا إِصْرًا كَمَا حَمَلْتَهُ عَلَى الَّذِينَ مِن قَبْلِنَا رَبَّنَا

وَلاَ تُحَمِّلْنَا مَا لاَ طَاقَةَ لَنَا بِهِ وَاعْفُ عَنَّا وَاغْفِرْ لَنَا وَارْحَمْنَآ أَنتَ مَوْلاَنَا فَانصُرْنَا عَلَى الْقَوْمِ

الْكَافِرِينَ

3:10 إِنَّ الَّذِينَ كَفَرُواْ لَن تُغْنِيَ عَنْهُمْ أَمْوَالُهُمْ وَلاَ أَوْلاَدُهُم مِّنَ اللهِ شَيْئًا وَأُوْلَئِكَ هُمْ وَقُودُ

النَّارِ

3:25 فَكَيْفَ إِذَا جَمَعْنَاهُمْ لِيَوْمٍ لاَّ رَيْبَ فِيهِ وَوُفِّيَتْ كُلُّ نَفْسٍ مَّا كَسَبَتْ وَهُمْ لاَ يُظْلَمُونَ

3:70 يَاأَهْلَ الْكِتَابِ لِمَ تَكْفُرُونَ بِآيَاتِ اللهِ وَأَنتُمْ تَشْهَدُونَ

3:71 يَا أَهْلَ الْكِتَابِ لِمَ تَلْبِسُونَ الْحَقَّ بِالْبَاطِلِ وَتَكْتُمُونَ الْحَقَّ وَأَنتُمْ تَعْلَمُونَ

3:102 يَا أَيُّهَا الَّذِينَ آمَنُواْ اتَّقُواْ اللهَ حَقَّ تُقَاتِهِ وَلاَ تَمُوتُنَّ إِلاَّ وَأَنتُم مُّسْلِمُونَ

3:103 وَاعْتَصِمُواْ بِحَبْلِ اللهِ جَمِيعًا وَلاَ تَفَرَّقُواْ وَاذْكُرُواْ نِعْمَةَ اللهِ عَلَيْكُمْ إِذْ كُنتُمْ أَعْدَاء

فَأَلَّفَ بَيْنَ قُلُوبِكُمْ فَأَصْبَحْتُم بِنِعْمَتِهِ إِخْوَانًا وَكُنتُمْ عَلَى شَفَا حُفْرَةٍ مِّنَ النَّارِ فَأَنقَذَكُم مِّنْهَا

كَذَلِكَ يُبَيِّنُ اللهُ لَكُمْ آيَاتِهِ لَعَلَّكُمْ تَهْتَدُونَ

3:104 وَلْتَكُن مِّنكُمْ أُمَّةٌ يَدْعُونَ إِلَى الْخَيْرِ وَيَأْمُرُونَ بِالْمَعْرُوفِ وَيَنْهَوْنَ عَنِ الْمُنكَرِ

وَأُوْلَئِكَ هُمُ الْمُفْلِحُونَ

3:105 وَلاَ تَكُونُواْ كَالَّذِينَ تَفَرَّقُواْ وَاخْتَلَفُواْ مِن بَعْدِ مَا جَاءهُمُ الْبَيِّنَاتُ وَأُوْلَئِكَ لَهُمْ عَذَابٌ عَظِيمٌ

3:113 لَيْسُواْ سَوَاء مِّنْ أَهْلِ الْكِتَابِ أُمَّةٌ قَآئِمَةٌ يَتْلُونَ آيَاتِ اللّهِ آنَاء اللَّيْلِ وَهُمْ يَسْجُدُونَ

3:114 يُؤْمِنُونَ بِاللّهِ وَالْيَوْمِ الآخِرِ وَيَأْمُرُونَ بِالْمَعْرُوفِ وَيَنْهَوْنَ عَنِ الْمُنكَرِ وَيُسَارِعُونَ فِي الْخَيْرَاتِ وَأُوْلَئِكَ مِنَ الصَّالِحِينَ

3:115 وَمَا يَفْعَلُواْ مِنْ خَيْرٍ فَلَن يُكْفَرُوْهُ وَاللّهُ عَلِيمٌ بِالْمُتَّقِينَ

3:133 وَسَارِعُواْ إِلَى مَغْفِرَةٍ مِّن رَّبِّكُمْ وَجَنَّةٍ عَرْضُهَا السَّمَاوَاتُ وَالأَرْضُ أُعِدَّتْ لِلْمُتَّقِينَ

3:135 وَالَّذِينَ إِذَا فَعَلُواْ فَاحِشَةً أَوْ ظَلَمُواْ أَنْفُسَهُمْ ذَكَرُواْ اللّهَ فَاسْتَغْفَرُواْ لِذُنُوبِهِمْ وَمَن يَغْفِرُ الذُّنُوبَ إِلاَّ اللّهُ وَلَمْ يُصِرُّواْ عَلَى مَا فَعَلُواْ وَهُمْ يَعْلَمُونَ

3:186 لَتُبْلَوُنَّ فِي أَمْوَالِكُمْ وَأَنفُسِكُمْ وَلَتَسْمَعُنَّ مِنَ الَّذِينَ أُوتُواْ الْكِتَابَ مِن قَبْلِكُمْ وَمِنَ الَّذِينَ أَشْرَكُواْ أَذًى كَثِيرًا وَإِن تَصْبِرُواْ وَتَتَّقُواْ فَإِنَّ ذَلِكَ مِنْ عَزْمِ الأُمُورِ

5:32 مِنْ أَجْلِ ذَلِكَ كَتَبْنَا عَلَى بَنِي إِسْرَائِيلَ أَنَّهُ مَن قَتَلَ نَفْسًا بِغَيْرِ نَفْسٍ أَوْ فَسَادٍ فِي الأَرْضِ فَكَأَنَّمَا قَتَلَ النَّاسَ جَمِيعًا وَمَنْ أَحْيَاهَا فَكَأَنَّمَا أَحْيَا النَّاسَ جَمِيعًا وَلَقَدْ جَاء تْهُمْ رُسُلُنَا بِالبَيِّنَاتِ ثُمَّ إِنَّ كَثِيرًا مِّنْهُم بَعْدَ ذَلِكَ فِي الأَرْضِ لَمُسْرِفُونَ

6:95 إِنَّ اللّهَ فَالِقُ الْحَبِّ وَالنَّوَى يُخْرِجُ الْحَيَّ مِنَ الْمَيِّتِ وَمُخْرِجُ الْمَيِّتِ مِنَ الْحَيِّ ذَلِكُمُ اللّهُ فَأَنَّى تُؤْفَكُونَ

199

6:96 فَالِقُ الإِصْبَاحِ وَجَعَلَ اللَّيْلَ سَكَنًا وَالشَّمْسَ وَالْقَمَرَ حُسْبَانًا ذَلِكَ تَقْدِيرُ الْعَزِيزِ

الْعَلِيمِ

6:97 وَهُوَ الَّذِي جَعَلَ لَكُمُ النُّجُومَ لِتَهْتَدُوا بِهَا فِي ظُلُمَاتِ الْبَرِّ وَالْبَحْرِ قَدْ فَصَّلْنَا الآيَاتِ

لِقَوْمٍ يَعْلَمُونَ

6:98 وَهُوَ الَّذِي أَنشَأَكُم مِّن نَّفْسٍ وَاحِدَةٍ فَمُسْتَقَرٌّ وَمُسْتَوْدَعٌ قَدْ فَصَّلْنَا الآيَاتِ لِقَوْمٍ

يَفْقَهُونَ

6:99 وَهُوَ الَّذِي أَنزَلَ مِنَ السَّمَاء مَاء فَأَخْرَجْنَا بِهِ نَبَاتَ كُلِّ شَيْءٍ فَأَخْرَجْنَا مِنْهُ خَضِرًا

نُّخْرِجُ مِنْهُ حَبًّا مُّتَرَاكِبًا وَمِنَ النَّخْلِ مِن طَلْعِهَا قِنْوَانٌ دَانِيَةٌ وَجَنَّاتٍ مِّنْ أَعْنَابٍ وَالزَّيْتُونَ

وَالرُّمَّانَ مُشْتَبِهًا وَغَيْرَ مُتَشَابِهٍ انظُرُواْ إِلَى ثَمَرِهِ إِذَا أَثْمَرَ وَيَنْعِهِ إِنَّ فِي ذَلِكُمْ لآيَاتٍ لِّقَوْمٍ يُؤْمِنُونَ

6:122 أَوَ مَن كَانَ مَيْتًا فَأَحْيَيْنَاهُ وَجَعَلْنَا لَهُ نُورًا يَمْشِي بِهِ فِي النَّاسِ كَمَن مَّثَلُهُ فِي

الظُّلُمَاتِ لَيْسَ بِخَارِجٍ مِّنْهَا كَذَلِكَ زُيِّنَ لِلْكَافِرِينَ مَا كَانُواْ يَعْمَلُونَ

6:151 قُلْ تَعَالَوْاْ أَتْلُ مَا حَرَّمَ رَبُّكُمْ عَلَيْكُمْ أَلاَّ تُشْرِكُواْ بِهِ شَيْئًا وَبِالْوَالِدَيْنِ إِحْسَانًا وَلاَ

تَقْتُلُواْ أَوْلاَدَكُم مِّنْ إمْلاَقٍ نَّحْنُ نَرْزُقُكُمْ وَإِيَّاهُمْ وَلاَ تَقْرَبُواْ الْفَوَاحِشَ مَا ظَهَرَ مِنْهَا وَمَا بَطَنَ

وَلاَ تَقْتُلُواْ النَّفْسَ الَّتِي حَرَّمَ اللهُ إِلاَّ بِالْحَقِّ ذَلِكُمْ وَصَّاكُمْ بِهِ لَعَلَّكُمْ تَعْقِلُونَ

6:152 وَلاَ تَقْرَبُواْ مَالَ الْيَتِيمِ إِلاَّ بِالَّتِي هِيَ أَحْسَنُ حَتَّى يَبْلُغَ أَشُدَّهُ وَأَوْفُواْ الْكَيْلَ

وَالْمِيزَانَ بِالْقِسْطِ لاَ نُكَلِّفُ نَفْسًا إِلاَّ وُسْعَهَا وَإِذَا قُلْتُمْ فَاعْدِلُواْ وَلَوْ كَانَ ذَا قُرْبَى وَبِعَهْدِ اللهِ

أَوْفُواْ ذَلِكُمْ وَصَّاكُم بِهِ لَعَلَّكُمْ تَذَكَّرُونَ

6:160 مَن جَاء بِالْحَسَنَةِ فَلَهُ عَشْرُ أَمْثَالِهَا وَمَن جَاء بِالسَّيِّئَةِ فَلاَ يُجْزَى إِلاَّ مِثْلَهَا وَهُمْ لاَ
يُظْلَمُونَ

7:27 يَا بَنِي آدَمَ لاَ يَفْتِنَنَّكُمُ الشَّيْطَانُ كَمَا أَخْرَجَ أَبَوَيْكُم مِّنَ الْجَنَّةِ يَنزِعُ عَنْهُمَا لِبَاسَهُمَا
لِيُرِيَهُمَا سَوْءَاتِهِمَا إِنَّهُ يَرَاكُمْ هُوَ وَقَبِيلُهُ مِنْ حَيْثُ لاَ تَرَوْنَهُمْ إِنَّا جَعَلْنَا الشَّيَاطِينَ أَوْلِيَاء لِلَّذِينَ
لاَ يُؤْمِنُونَ

7:33 قُلْ إِنَّمَا حَرَّمَ رَبِّيَ الْفَوَاحِشَ مَا ظَهَرَ مِنْهَا وَمَا بَطَنَ وَالإِثْمَ وَالْبَغْيَ بِغَيْرِ الْحَقِّ وَأَن
تُشْرِكُواْ بِاللّهِ مَا لَمْ يُنَزِّلْ بِهِ سُلْطَانًا وَأَن تَقُولُواْ عَلَى اللّهِ مَا لاَ تَعْلَمُونَ

7:175 وَاتْلُ عَلَيْهِمْ نَبَأَ الَّذِيَ آتَيْنَاهُ آيَاتِنَا فَانسَلَخَ مِنْهَا فَأَتْبَعَهُ الشَّيْطَانُ فَكَانَ مِنَ
الْغَاوِينَ

7:176 وَلَوْ شِئْنَا لَرَفَعْنَاهُ بِهَا وَلَكِنَّهُ أَخْلَدَ إِلَى الأَرْضِ وَاتَّبَعَ هَوَاهُ فَمَثَلُهُ كَمَثَلِ الْكَلْبِ إِن
تَحْمِلْ عَلَيْهِ يَلْهَثْ أَوْ تَتْرُكْهُ يَلْهَث ذَّلِكَ مَثَلُ الْقَوْمِ الَّذِينَ كَذَّبُواْ بِآيَاتِنَا فَاقْصُصِ الْقَصَصَ
لَعَلَّهُمْ يَتَفَكَّرُونَ

8:2 إِنَّمَا الْمُؤْمِنُونَ الَّذِينَ إِذَا ذُكِرَ اللّهُ وَجِلَتْ قُلُوبُهُمْ وَإِذَا تُلِيَتْ عَلَيْهِمْ آيَاتُهُ زَادَتْهُمْ إِيمَانًا
وَعَلَى رَبِّهِمْ يَتَوَكَّلُونَ

9:18 إِنَّمَا يَعْمُرُ مَسَاجِدَ اللّهِ مَنْ آمَنَ بِاللّهِ وَالْيَوْمِ الآخِرِ وَأَقَامَ الصَّلاَةَ وَآتَى الزَّكَاةَ وَلَمْ
يَخْشَ إِلاَّ اللّهَ فَعَسَى أُوْلَئِكَ أَن يَكُونُواْ مِنَ الْمُهْتَدِينَ

9:34 يَا أَيُّهَا الَّذِينَ آمَنُواْ إِنَّ كَثِيرًا مِّنَ الأَحْبَارِ وَالرُّهْبَانِ لَيَأْكُلُونَ أَمْوَالَ النَّاسِ بِالْبَاطِلِ وَيَصُدُّونَ عَن سَبِيلِ اللهِ وَالَّذِينَ يَكْنِزُونَ الذَّهَبَ وَالْفِضَّةَ وَلاَ يُنفِقُونَهَا فِي سَبِيلِ اللهِ فَبَشِّرْهُم بِعَذَابٍ أَلِيمٍ

9:35 يَوْمَ يُحْمَى عَلَيْهَا فِي نَارِ جَهَنَّمَ فَتُكْوَى بِهَا جِبَاهُهُمْ وَجُنوبُهُمْ وَظُهُورُهُمْ هَذَا مَا كَنَزْتُمْ لأَنفُسِكُمْ فَذُوقُواْ مَا كُنتُمْ تَكْنِزُونَ

9:40 إِلاَّ تَنصُرُوهُ فَقَدْ نَصَرَهُ اللهُ إِذْ أَخْرَجَهُ الَّذِينَ كَفَرُواْ ثَانِيَ اثْنَيْنِ إِذْ هُمَا فِي الْغَارِ إِذْ يَقُولُ لِصَاحِبِهِ لاَ تَحْزَنْ إِنَّ اللهَ مَعَنَا فَأَنزَلَ اللهُ سَكِينَتَهُ عَلَيْهِ وَأَيَّدَهُ بِجُنُودٍ لَّمْ تَرَوْهَا وَجَعَلَ كَلِمَةَ الَّذِينَ كَفَرُواْ السُّفْلَى وَكَلِمَةُ اللهِ هِيَ الْعُلْيَا وَاللهُ عَزِيزٌ حَكِيمٌ

9:60 إِنَّمَا الصَّدَقَاتُ لِلْفُقَرَاء وَالْمَسَاكِينِ وَالْعَامِلِينَ عَلَيْهَا وَالْمُؤَلَّفَةِ قُلُوبُهُمْ وَفِي الرِّقَابِ وَالْغَارِمِينَ وَفِي سَبِيلِ اللهِ وَابْنِ السَّبِيلِ فَرِيضَةً مِّنَ اللهِ وَاللهُ عَلِيمٌ حَكِيمٌ

9:75 وَمِنْهُم مَّنْ عَاهَدَ اللهَ لَئِنْ آتَانَا مِن فَضْلِهِ لَنَصَّدَّقَنَّ وَلَنَكُونَنَّ مِنَ الصَّالِحِينَ

9:76 فَلَمَّا آتَاهُم مِّن فَضْلِهِ بَخِلُواْ بِهِ وَتَوَلَّواْ وَّهُم مُّعْرِضُونَ

9:79 الَّذِينَ يَلْمِزُونَ الْمُطَّوِّعِينَ مِنَ الْمُؤْمِنِينَ فِي الصَّدَقَاتِ وَالَّذِينَ لاَ يَجِدُونَ إِلاَّ جُهْدَهُمْ فَيَسْخَرُونَ مِنْهُمْ سَخِرَ اللهُ مِنْهُمْ وَلَهُمْ عَذَابٌ أَلِيمٌ

10:24 إِنَّمَا مَثَلُ الْحَيَاةِ الدُّنْيَا كَمَاء أَنزَلْنَاهُ مِنَ السَّمَاء فَاخْتَلَطَ بِهِ نَبَاتُ الأَرْضِ مِمَّا يَأْكُلُ النَّاسُ وَالأَنْعَامُ حَتَّى إِذَا أَخَذَتِ الأَرْضُ زُخْرُفَهَا وَازَّيَّنَتْ وَظَنَّ أَهْلُهَا أَنَّهُمْ قَادِرُونَ عَلَيْهَا أَتَاهَا أَمْرُنَا لَيْلاً أَوْ نَهَارًا فَجَعَلْنَاهَا حَصِيدًا كَأَن لَّمْ تَغْنَ بِالأَمْسِ كَذَلِكَ نُفَصِّلُ الآيَاتِ لِقَوْمٍ يَتَفَكَّرُونَ

10:35-36قُلْ هَلْ مِن شُرَكَآئِكُم مَّن يَهْدِي إِلَى الْحَقِّ قُلِ اللهُ يَهْدِي لِلْحَقِّ أَفَمَن يَهْدِي إِلَى الْحَقِّ أَحَقُّ أَن يُتَّبَعَ أَمَّن لاَّ يَهِدِّيَ إِلاَّ أَن يُهْدَى فَمَا لَكُمْ كَيْفَ تَحْكُمُونَ وَمَا يَتَّبِعُ أَكْثَرُهُمْ إِلاَّ ظَنًّا إِنَّ الظَّنَّ لاَ يُغْنِي مِنَ الْحَقِّ شَيْئًا إِنَّ اللّهَ عَلَيمٌ بِمَا يَفْعَلُونَ

10:107وَإِن يَمْسَسْكَ اللّهُ بِضُرٍّ فَلاَ كَاشِفَ لَهُ إِلاَّ هُوَ وَإِن يُرِدْكَ بِخَيْرٍ فَلاَ رَآدَّ لِفَضْلِهِ يُصَيبُ بِهِ مَن يَشَاء مِنْ عِبَادِهِ وَهُوَ الْغَفُورُ الرَّحِيمُ

11:100ذَلِكَ مِنْ أَنبَاء الْقُرَى نَقُصُّهُ عَلَيْكَ مِنْهَا قَآئِمٌ وَحَصِيدٌ

12:3نَحْنُ نَقُصُّ عَلَيْكَ أَحْسَنَ الْقَصَصِ بِمَا أَوْحَيْنَا إِلَيْكَ هَذَا الْقُرْآنَ وَإِن كُنتَ مِن قَبْلِهِ لَمِنَ الْغَافِلِينَ

13:11لَهُ مُعَقِّبَاتٌ مِّن بَيْنِ يَدَيْهِ وَمِنْ خَلْفِهِ يَحْفَظُونَهُ مِنْ أَمْرِ اللّهِ إِنَّ اللّهَ لاَ يُغَيِّرُ مَا بِقَوْمٍ حَتَّى يُغَيِّرُواْ مَا بِأَنْفُسِهِمْ وَإِذَا أَرَادَ اللّهُ بِقَوْمٍ سُوءًا فَلاَ مَرَدَّ لَهُ وَمَا لَهُم مِّن دُونِهِ مِن وَالٍ

13:28الَّذِينَ آمَنُواْ وَتَطْمَئِنُّ قُلُوبُهُم بِذِكْرِ اللّهِ أَلاَ بِذِكْرِ اللّهِ تَطْمَئِنُّ الْقُلُوبُ

14:21وَبَرَزُواْ لِلّهِ جَمِيعًا فَقَالَ الضُّعَفَاء لِلَّذِينَ اسْتَكْبَرُواْ إِنَّا كُنَّا لَكُمْ تَبَعًا فَهَلْ أَنتُم مُّغْنُونَ عَنَّا مِنْ عَذَابِ اللّهِ مِن شَيْءٍ قَالُواْ لَوْ هَدَانَا اللّهُ لَهَدَيْنَاكُمْ سَوَاء عَلَيْنَآ أَجَزِعْنَا أَمْ صَبَرْنَا مَا لَنَا مِن مَّحِيصٍ

14:22وَقَالَ الشَّيْطَانُ لَمَّا قُضِيَ الأَمْرُ إِنَّ اللّهَ وَعَدَكُمْ وَعْدَ الْحَقِّ وَوَعَدتُّكُمْ فَأَخْلَفْتُكُمْ وَمَا كَانَ لِيَ عَلَيْكُم مِّن سُلْطَانٍ إِلاَّ أَن دَعَوْتُكُمْ فَاسْتَجَبْتُمْ لِي فَلاَ تَلُومُونِي وَلُومُواْ أَنفُسَكُم مَّا أَنَاْ بِمُصْرِخِكُمْ وَمَا أَنتُمْ بِمُصْرِخِيَّ إِنِّي كَفَرْتُ بِمَا أَشْرَكْتُمُونِ مِن قَبْلُ إِنَّ الظَّالِمِينَ لَهُمْ عَذَابٌ أَلِيمٌ

203

14:31 قُل لِّعِبَادِيَ الَّذِينَ آمَنُواْ يُقِيمُواْ الصَّلاَةَ وَيُنفِقُواْ مِمَّا رَزَقْنَاهُمْ سِرًّا وَعَلانِيَةً مِّن قَبْلِ أَن يَأْتِيَ يَوْمٌ لاَّ بَيْعٌ فِيهِ وَلاَ خِلاَلٌ

14:34 وَآتَاكُم مِّن كُلِّ مَا سَأَلْتُمُوهُ وَإِن تَعُدُّواْ نِعْمَتَ اللّهِ لاَ تُحْصُوهَا إِنَّ الإِنسَانَ لَظَلُومٌ كَفَّارٌ

14:47 فَلاَ تَحْسَبَنَّ اللّهَ مُخْلِفَ وَعْدِهِ رُسُلَهُ إِنَّ اللّهَ عَزِيزٌ ذُو انتِقَامٍ

15:3 ذَرْهُمْ يَأْكُلُواْ وَيَتَمَتَّعُواْ وَيُلْهِهِمُ الأَمَلُ فَسَوْفَ يَعْلَمُونَ

15:8 مَا نُنَزِّلُ الْمَلائِكَةَ إِلاَّ بِالحَقِّ وَمَا كَانُواْ إِذًا مُّنظَرِينَ

15:9 إِنَّا نَحْنُ نَزَّلْنَا الذِّكْرَ وَإِنَّا لَهُ لَحَافِظُونَ

15:80 وَلَقَدْ كَذَّبَ أَصْحَابُ الحِجْرِ الْمُرْسَلِينَ

16:44 بِالْبَيِّنَاتِ وَالزُّبُرِ وَأَنزَلْنَا إِلَيْكَ الذِّكْرَ لِتُبَيِّنَ لِلنَّاسِ مَا نُزِّلَ إِلَيْهِمْ وَلَعَلَّهُمْ يَتَفَكَّرُونَ

20:38-39 إِذْ أَوْحَيْنَا إِلَى أُمِّكَ مَا يُوحَى أَنِ اقْذِفِيهِ فِي التَّابُوتِ فَاقْذِفِيهِ فِي الْيَمِّ فَلْيُلْقِهِ الْيَمُّ بِالسَّاحِلِ يَأْخُذْهُ عَدُوٌّ لِّي وَعَدُوٌّ لَّهُ وَأَلْقَيْتُ عَلَيْكَ مَحَبَّةً مِّنِّي وَلِتُصْنَعَ عَلَى عَيْنِي وَعَلَى كُلِّ ضَامِرٍ يَأْتِينَ مِن كُلِّ فَجٍّ عَمِيقٍ

20:77 وَلَقَدْ أَوْحَيْنَا إِلَى مُوسَى أَنْ أَسْرِ بِعِبَادِي فَاضْرِبْ لَهُمْ طَرِيقًا فِي الْبَحْرِ يَبَسًا لاَّ تَخَافُ دَرَكًا وَلاَ تَخْشَى

22:11 وَمِنَ النَّاسِ مَن يَعْبُدُ اللَّهَ عَلَى حَرْفٍ فَإِنْ أَصَابَهُ خَيْرٌ اطْمَأَنَّ بِهِ وَإِنْ أَصَابَتْهُ فِتْنَةٌ انقَلَبَ عَلَى وَجْهِهِ خَسِرَ الدُّنْيَا وَالآخِرَةَ ذَلِكَ هُوَ الْخُسْرَانُ الْمُبِينُ

22:27 وَأَذِّن فِي النَّاسِ بِالْحَجِّ يَأْتُوكَ رِجَالاً

24:35 اللَّهُ نُورُ السَّمَاوَاتِ وَالْأَرْضِ مَثَلُ نُورِهِ كَمِشْكَاةٍ فِيهَا مِصْبَاحٌ الْمِصْبَاحُ فِي زُجَاجَةٍ

الزُّجَاجَةُ كَأَنَّهَا كَوْكَبٌ دُرِّيٌّ يُوقَدُ مِن شَجَرَةٍ مُبَارَكَةٍ زَيْتُونِةٍ لَّا شَرْقِيَّةٍ وَلَا غَرْبِيَّةٍ يَكَادُ زَيْتُهَا

يُضِيءُ وَلَوْ لَمْ تَمْسَسْهُ نَارٌ نُّورٌ عَلَى نُورٍ يَهْدِي اللَّهُ لِنُورِهِ مَن يَشَاء وَيَضْرِبُ اللَّهُ الْأَمْثَالَ لِلنَّاسِ

وَاللَّهُ بِكُلِّ شَيْءٍ عَلِيمٌ

25:23 وَقَدِمْنَا إِلَى مَا عَمِلُوا مِنْ عَمَلٍ فَجَعَلْنَاهُ هَبَاء مَّنثُورًا

25:42 إِن كَادَ لَيُضِلُّنَا عَنْ آلِهَتِنَا لَوْلَا أَن صَبَرْنَا عَلَيْهَا وَسَوْفَ يَعْلَمُونَ حِينَ يَرَوْنَ

الْعَذَابَ مَنْ أَضَلُّ سَبِيلًا

25:43 أَرَأَيْتَ مَنِ اتَّخَذَ إِلَهَهُ هَوَاهُ أَفَأَنتَ تَكُونُ عَلَيْهِ وَكِيلًا

25:45-49 أَلَمْ تَرَ إِلَى رَبِّكَ كَيْفَ مَدَّ الظِّلَّ وَلَوْ شَاء لَجَعَلَهُ سَاكِنًا ثُمَّ جَعَلْنَا الشَّمْسَ

عَلَيْهِ دَلِيلًا ثُمَّ قَبَضْنَاهُ إِلَيْنَا قَبْضًا يَسِيرًا وَهُوَ الَّذِي جَعَلَ لَكُمُ اللَّيْلَ لِبَاسًا وَالنَّوْمَ سُبَاتًا وَجَعَلَ

النَّهَارَ نُشُورًا وَهُوَ الَّذِي أَرْسَلَ الرِّيَاحَ بُشْرًا بَيْنَ يَدَيْ رَحْمَتِهِ وَأَنزَلْنَا مِنَ السَّمَاء مَاء

طَهُورًا لِنُحْيِيَ بِهِ بَلْدَةً مَّيْتًا وَنُسْقِيَهُ مِمَّا خَلَقْنَا أَنْعَامًا وَأَنَاسِيَّ كَثِيرًا

25:63 وَعِبَادُ الرَّحْمَنِ الَّذِينَ يَمْشُونَ عَلَى الْأَرْضِ هَوْنًا وَإِذَا خَاطَبَهُمُ الْجَاهِلُونَ قَالُوا

سَلَامًا

28:11 وَقَالَتْ لِأُخْتِهِ قُصِّيهِ فَبَصُرَتْ بِهِ عَن جُنُبٍ وَهُمْ لَا يَشْعُرُونَ

30:9 أَوَلَمْ يَسِيرُوا فِي الْأَرْضِ فَيَنظُرُوا كَيْفَ كَانَ عَاقِبَةُ الَّذِينَ مِن قَبْلِهِمْ كَانُوا أَشَدَّ مِنْهُمْ

قُوَّةً وَأَثَارُوا الْأَرْضَ وَعَمَرُوهَا أَكْثَرَ مِمَّا عَمَرُوهَا وَجَاءتْهُمْ رُسُلُهُم بِالْبَيِّنَاتِ فَمَا كَانَ اللَّهُ

لِيَظْلِمَهُمْ وَلَكِن كَانُوا أَنفُسَهُمْ يَظْلِمُونَ

32:15 إِنَّمَا يُؤْمِنُ بِآيَاتِنَا الَّذِينَ إِذَا ذُكِّرُوا بِهَا خَرُّوا سُجَّدًا وَسَبَّحُوا بِحَمْدِ رَبِّهِمْ وَهُمْ لَا يَسْتَكْبِرُونَ

32:24 وَجَعَلْنَا مِنْهُمْ أَئِمَّةً يَهْدُونَ بِأَمْرِنَا لَمَّا صَبَرُوا وَكَانُوا بِآيَاتِنَا يُوقِنُونَ

33:21 لَقَدْ كَانَ لَكُمْ فِي رَسُولِ اللهِ أُسْوَةٌ حَسَنَةٌ لِمَن كَانَ يَرْجُو اللهَ وَالْيَوْمَ الْآخِرَ وَذَكَرَ اللهَ كَثِيرًا

35:11 وَاللهُ خَلَقَكُم مِّن تُرَابٍ ثُمَّ مِن نُّطْفَةٍ ثُمَّ جَعَلَكُمْ أَزْوَاجًا وَمَا تَحْمِلُ مِنْ أُنثَى وَلَا تَضَعُ إِلَّا بِعِلْمِهِ وَمَا يُعَمَّرُ مِن مُّعَمَّرٍ وَلَا يُنقَصُ مِنْ عُمُرِهِ إِلَّا فِي كِتَابٍ إِنَّ ذَلِكَ عَلَى اللهِ يَسِيرٌ

40:68 هُوَ الَّذِي يُحْيِي وَيُمِيتُ فَإِذَا قَضَى أَمْرًا فَإِنَّمَا يَقُولُ لَهُ كُن فَيَكُونُ

41:43 مَا يُقَالُ لَكَ إِلَّا مَا قَدْ قِيلَ لِلرُّسُلِ مِن قَبْلِكَ إِنَّ رَبَّكَ لَذُو مَغْفِرَةٍ وَذُو عِقَابٍ أَلِيمٍ

43:35 وَزُخْرُفًا وَإِن كُلُّ ذَلِكَ لَمَّا مَتَاعُ الْحَيَاةِ الدُّنْيَا وَالْآخِرَةُ عِندَ رَبِّكَ لِلْمُتَّقِينَ

44:10 فَارْتَقِبْ يَوْمَ تَأْتِي السَّمَاءُ بِدُخَانٍ مُّبِينٍ

47:24 أَفَلَا يَتَدَبَّرُونَ الْقُرْآنَ أَمْ عَلَى قُلُوبٍ أَقْفَالُهَا

51:56 وَمَا خَلَقْتُ الْجِنَّ وَالْإِنسَ إِلَّا لِيَعْبُدُونِ

53:29 فَأَعْرِضْ عَن مَّن تَوَلَّى عَن ذِكْرِنَا وَلَمْ يُرِدْ إِلَّا الْحَيَاةَ الدُّنْيَا

54:17 وَلَقَدْ يَسَّرْنَا الْقُرْآنَ لِلذِّكْرِ فَهَلْ مِن مُّدَّكِرٍ

61:8 يُرِيدُونَ لِيُطْفِئُوا نُورَ اللهِ بِأَفْوَاهِهِمْ وَاللهُ مُتِمُّ نُورِهِ وَلَوْ كَرِهَ الْكَافِرُونَ

About the Authors

Mohamed Hag Magid

Imam Mohamed Hag Magid is currently the Imam and Executive Director of the All Dulles Area Muslim Society (ADAMS) Center in Sterling, VA, and president of Islamic Society of North America (ISNA). He was born in Sudan, the son of a leading Islamic Scholar, who was an Azhar graduate and the President of the Supreme Council of Islamic Affairs in Sudan. Imam Magid studied at the hand of his father and other notable scholars, gaining ijaza in several disciplines, including Ghazali's Ihya-Uloom-al-Deen. He has also served as chair of Faith Communities in Action (Virginia), member of InterFaith Conference of Metropolitan Washington Assembly, and a former board member of Fairfax Youth Partnership.

Hanaa Unus

Hanaa Unus holds a Master's degree student in Islamic studies from Hartford Seminary. She earned a Bachelors of Science in Social Work from George Mason University. Unus has also served as national president of the Muslim Youth of North America (MYNA).

ADDITIONAL NOTES

ADDITIONAL NOTES

ADDITIONAL NOTES

Made in the USA
Charleston, SC
04 June 2014